• CELEBRATING HOLIDAYS & FESTIVALS AROUND THE WORLD •

Ramadan

Betsy Richardson

MASON CREST

Mason Crest
450 Parkway Drive, Suite D Broomall, PA 19008
www.masoncrest.com

Printed in the United States of America
First printing
9 8 7 6 5 4 3 2 1

Series ISBN: 978-1-4222-4143-1
Hardcover ISBN: 978-1-4222-4150-9

Library of Congress Cataloging-in-Publication Data is available on file.

Developed and Produced by Print Matters Productions, Inc. (www.printmattersinc.com)
Cover and Interior Design by Lori S Malkin Design LLC

KEY ICONS TO LOOK FOR:

 Words to understand: These words with their easy-to-understand definitions will increase the reader's understanding of the text while building vocabulary skills.

 Sidebars: This boxed material within the main text allows readers to build knowledge, gain insights, explore possibilities, and broaden their perspectives by weaving together additional information to provide realistic and holistic perspectives.

 Educational Videos: Readers can view videos by scanning our QR codes, providing them with additional educational content to supplement the text. Examples include news coverage, moments in history, speeches, iconic sports moments and much more!

 Text-dependent Questions: These questions send the reader back to the text for more careful attention to the evidence presented there.

 Research projects: Readers are pointed toward areas of further inquiry connected to each chapter. Suggestions are provided for projects that encourage deeper research and analysis.

 Series glossary of key terms: This back-of-the book glossary contains terminology used throughout this series. Words found here increase the reader's ability to read and comprehend higher-level books and articles in this field.

CONTENTS

INTRODUCTION

Celebrating Holidays & Festivals Around the World

Holidays mark time. They occupy a space outside of ordinary events and give shape and meaning to our everyday existence. They also remind us of the passage of time as we reflect on Christmases, Passovers, or Ramadans past. Throughout human history, nations and peoples have marked their calendars with special days to celebrate, commemorate, and memorialize. We set aside times to reflect on the past and future, to rest and renew physically and spiritually, and to simply have fun.

In English we call these extraordinary moments "holidays," a contraction of the term "holy day." Sometimes holidays are truly holy days–the Sabbath, Easter, or Eid al-Fitr, for example–but they can also be nonreligious occasions that serve political purposes, address the social needs of communities and individuals, or focus on regional customs and games.

This series explores the meanings and celebrations of holidays across religions and cultures around the world. It groups the holidays into volumes according to theme (such as *Lent, Yom Kippur & Days of Repentance; Thanksgiving & Other Festivals of the Harvest; Independence Days; Easter, Passover & Festivals of Hope; Ringing in the Western & Chinese New Year; Marking the Religious New Year; Carnival; Ramadan;* and *Halloween & Remembrances of the Dead*) or by their common human experience due to their closeness on the calendar (such as *Christmas & Hanukkah*). Each volume introduces readers to the origins, history, and common practices associated with the holidays before embarking on a worldwide tour that shows the regional variations and distinctive celebrations within specific countries. The reader will learn how these holidays started, what they mean to the people who celebrate them, and how different cultures celebrate them.

▲ Muslims select traditional dishes at a Ramadan bazaar in downtown Kuala Lumpur, Malaysia, during the holy month of Ramadan.

These volumes have an international focus, and thus readers will be able to learn about diversity both at home and throughout the world. We can learn a great deal about a people or nation by the holidays they celebrate. We can also learn from holidays how cultures and religions have interacted and mingled over time. We see in celebrations not just the past through tradition, but the principles and traits that people embrace and value today.

The Celebrating Holidays & Festivals Around the World series surveys this rich and varied festive terrain. Its 10 volumes show the distinct ways that people all over the world infuse ordinary life with meaning, purpose, or joy. The series cannot be all-inclusive or the last word on so vast a subject, but it offers a vital first step for those eager to learn more about the diverse, fascinating, and vibrant cultures of the world, through the festivities that give expression, order, and meaning to their lives.

INTRODUCTION

Ramadan

Ramadan, also known as Ramzan, is a holiday marked by contrast. While traditionally a sacred period devoted to prayer, fasting, and charity, Ramadan has more recently become an occasion for many Muslims to feast, party, and shop. The most enthusiastic feasting often occurs during the holiday Eid al-Fitr, the "Festival of the Breaking of the Fast" that ends Ramadan every year.

Ramadan is celebrated by Muslims across the world who remain true to the ceremony's Middle Eastern origins while incorporating elements drawn from the cultures of their new homelands. If you asked Muslims from Saudi Arabia, Michigan, and New Zealand what they appreciate about Ramadan, many would give similar answers. They would mention the spiritual strength they feel as they fast and pray, and the sense of community they enjoy while celebrating the end of the fast each evening. In many countries they might also mention parties, gifts, and new clothes. In Islamic regions, Muslims decorate their shops and homes, and excitement is in the air. Even in countries with few Muslims, Ramadan is a much-anticipated time to focus on faith, family, and feasting.

▲ Muslim faithful visit the Dome of the Rock in Jerusalem. During Ramadan, worshippers pray outside the Dome of the Rock on the first Friday. More than 100,000 people take part in the prayers at the Al-Aqsa Mosque compound.

Origins of Ramadan

Muslims practice a religion called Islam. Like Christianity and Judaism, Islam is an **Abrahamic** religion, which means that Muslims believe that the patriarch Abraham in the book of Genesis was one of the founders of the religion. All three religions share belief in one God. Islam is the youngest of these religions, originating in the 600s.

■ The Creation of Islam

The man responsible for the creation of Islam as a religion was called Muhammad. He is not considered the founder of Islam, because Muslims believe that he simply used the teachings of **Allah**, or God, to restore purity to an existing faith that had been corrupted by Christians and Jews.

WORDS TO UNDERSTAND

Abrahamic: Used to describe a group of religions that recognize Abraham as a patriarch; this includes Judaism, Christianity, and Islam.
Allah: The Arabic word for God.
Caliph: The leader of the Islamic religion; this role does not exist anymore.
Pilgrimage: A journey made to a sacred place as an act of religious devotion.

◀ Hundreds of thousands of pilgrims perform Friday prayers at the great mosque in Mecca, Saudi Arabia. Pilgrims stream into Islam's holy city for the annual pilgrimage, which all able-bodied Muslim men are expected to make once in their lives.

◄ Muslim children read the Quran at a mosque before Ramadan night prayer, which marks the start of the Muslim fasting month.

According to Islamic tradition, Muhammad was the final prophet to whom God spoke. Through the angel Gabriel God gave Muhammad spiritual guidance in the form of scriptures known as the Quran, which became the main religious book of Islam. It took Gabriel 23 years to finish revealing these scriptures to Muhammad, but the process of transmitting the text began during the month of Ramadan.

THE FIVE PILLARS OF ISLAM

All Muslims are required to perform five duties, known as the Five Pillars of Islam. They must

- testify that there is no god but Allah and that Muhammad is his prophet
- pray five times a day
- give alms, or charitable contributions, to the poor
- fast during Ramadan
- make a **pilgrimage** to the city of Mecca once in their lives

■ The Importance of Ramadan

Muslims believe that the gates to heaven are open during Ramadan: Good deeds are richly rewarded and it is easier to enter heaven than other times of the year. Simultaneously the gates of hell are said to be closed and all devils chained up behind them. The devils are not loose to lure people into trouble, so it is especially easy to do good deeds instead of bad ones.

Believers try to pray more than usual during Ramadan in order to become even better Muslims. According to Islamic teaching, prayer functions as a

Get some fast facts on Ramadan.

way of fulfilling the needs of the spirit, just as food, water, and exercise fulfill the needs of the body. Prayer puts believers in touch with God, helping them remember his greatness and think of ways they can develop good qualities in themselves. Prayer is an opportunity to think about one's life and see how one's actions meet with God's desires.

Most Muslims make an effort to give up their bad habits during Ramadan. In particular, people try to avoid disagreements and anger, instead keeping positive, pleasant thoughts in their heads at all times.

■ Sunni and Shii Muslims

Muslims today are divided into two main groups, the Sunnis and the Shiis, that formed soon after the founding of Islam in the early 600s. When the prophet Muhammad died in 632, he left behind close to 100,000 Muslims without a leader. They did not all agree on who should succeed Muhammad.

One group elected Abu Bakr, a close friend and father-in-law of Muhammad, as the next leader, or **caliph**. Another group believed that Muhammad's son-in-law, Ali ibn Abi Talib, should be the caliph. Ali accepted Abu Bakr as caliph and Abu Bakr was the leader of Islam until his death in 634. Twenty-two years after Abu Bakr's death, Ali became the fourth caliph of Islam. (There were two other caliphs between Abu Bakr and Ali, Umar ibn al-Khattab and Uthman ibn Affan.) Some of Ali's original opponents still resisted his leadership, however, and eventually the conflict grew into a civil war.

The two groups split into religious factions. The supporters of Abu Bakr became known as Sunni, or "one who follows the Sunna." ("Sunna" are the words and actions of Prophet Muhammad.) The supporters of Ali became Shii, "supporters of Ali." Sunni Islam is now the largest denomination of Islam. Sunni Muslims live throughout the Middle East, Central Asia, North Africa, and Southeast Asia. Between 10 and 15 percent of Muslims are Shii. Most of them live in the Middle East, especially in Iran. Both groups believe in the Five Pillars of Islam, but they differ on various specifics, including when to start and end Ramadan.

▲ Muslims in India wait to break their fast at sunset during the month of Ramadan.

■ The Islamic Calendar

Islam uses a lunar calendar, based on the cycles of the Moon. Because the Moon goes through a complete cycle in 29 or 30 days, lunar months do not match up with the months of the Western Gregorian calendar. A lunar year has 354 days, instead of the 365 or 366 of the Gregorian calendar. Ramadan, or Ramzan, is the ninth month of the Islamic calendar. Each year, Ramadan starts 11 or 12 days earlier than it did the previous year. It takes about 33 Islamic years for the month to return to the same place in the Gregorian calendar.

Muslims throughout the world believe Ramadan is the holiest month of the year, a time to renew their spiritual commitment to their religion. Ramadan is sacred because Muslims believe that this was the month during which Allah revealed the Quran, the sacred book of Islam, to the prophet Muhammad. Muslims fast, which means they do not eat or drink during daylight hours, and they pray many times every day. They also try to give money to the poor. Though Ramadan can be serious and somber, it is also a time of festivities. Every night people eat great feasts to make up for not eating during the day. At the end of Ramadan, Muslims celebrate Eid al-Fitr.

BEGINNING ON THE NEW MOON

According to the Quran, Ramadan begins when the new Moon is visible to the naked eye. This narrow crescent Moon, which rises in the morning and sets in the evening, is nearly invisible, appearing in the west only just after sunset. Muslim children look expectantly for the sliver of a Moon, just as Christian children count the days until Christmas.

According to tradition, two witnesses must agree that the new Moon is visible and report this information to an Islamic leader called a *qadi*. If the *qadi* agrees, he reports to another religious leader called a *mufti*. The mufti announces to the community of believers that Ramadan has begun and the people begin their fast. This same procedure is used to determine that Ramadan has officially ended and that the time has come to break the fast and celebrate Eid al-Fitr. If the Moon is invisible at the beginning or end of the month, then the previous month is set at 30 days and Ramadan begins or ends when the 30th day ends.

Of course, the new Moon is not necessarily visible on the same day around the world because some areas may have clouds while others do not. In today's world, many Muslims let the mufti of Cairo, Egypt, make the determination of when Ramadan begins and ends so that all Muslims can observe Ramadan at the same time. Others consider Saudi Arabia the ultimate authority. In 2006, for example, Ramadan began on a

UTILIZING TECHNOLOGY

In some places, technology has trumped human observation. The Fiqh Council, a governing body of Muslims in North America, now uses astronomical instruments and calculations to decide when to begin and end Ramadan. In Saudi Arabia, observers sometimes go up in airplanes to look for the Moon.

ISLAMIC RELIGIOUS LEADERS

There are several different religious leaders in Islam:

- **ayatollah:** a major religious leader, scholar, and teacher in Shii Islam.
- **caliph:** the leader of the Islamic religion; does not exist anymore.
- **imam:** a leader; a scholar of Islam; the head of a mosque.
- **muezzin:** a person who issues the daily and weekly calls to prayer from a mosque.
- **mufti:** a scholar of Islamic law.
- **mullah:** a clergyman who is an expert on the Quran and religious matters.
- ***qadi:*** a judge in a Muslim community who upholds Islamic law.

▲ A local Muslim leader in Jakarta, Indonesia, uses a telescope on top of a communications tower to scan the skies in search of the new Moon. When the Moon is sighted, the king proclaims the beginning of the fasting month of Ramadan.

RAMADAN E-CARDS

In a modern twist on the Ramadan greeting cards Muslims traditionally send to family and friends, some Muslims send Ramadan e-cards that they find on various Web sites.

Saturday in Saudi Arabia and the United Arab Emirates, but on Sunday in Egypt, Jordan, and Syria. In Lebanon that year, Sunni Muslims began observing Ramadan on Saturday, while Shii Muslims waited to begin observing on Sunday.

The last 10 days of Ramadan are a period of particular spiritual importance because, Muslims believe, it was during this time that the very first verse of the Quran was revealed to Muhammad. This event happened on a night known as Laylat al-Qadr, or the "Night of Decree." Muslims know that Laylat al-Qadr occurs during the last 10 days of Ramadan, but no one knows exactly which night it is. According to Islamic tradition, Muhammad and God chose to keep the exact night secret so that believers would not pray only on that night. Instead they have to pray all 10 nights so as not to miss the event. Most of their prayers consist of lengthy recitations of the Quran. Some Muslims spend the last 10 days of Ramadan at the mosque, praying and reading the Quran all day long. This is a period of seclusion called *itikaf*.

TEXT-DEPENDENT QUESTIONS

1: Who is the man responsible for the creation of Islam as a religion?

2: What are the two main groups of Muslims?

3: What type of calendar does Islam use?

RESEARCH PROJECTS

1: Research the basic architecture of a mosque, including different styles, key features and decorative elements, and other details. Write a brief report summarizing your findings, including examples of some of the famous mosques of the world and their notable architectural elements.

2: Research some of the key works of Islamic literature, such as sacred texts like the Quran and the Hadith, poetry such as the *Kitab al-Aghani*, and philosophical or scientific works such as the *Kitab al-Hayawan*. Select a few of these works and create capsule summaries for each, including when they were written and how they influenced Islamic literature as a whole.

Observing Ramadan

Muslims observe several special practices during Ramadan that are meant to help them become more disciplined, improve their relationships with fellow Muslims, become closer to Allah, and gain greater empathy for the poor.

■ Hungry and Thirsty Days

The most important practice of Ramadan is fasting. The practice of fasting under Islamic law is called *sawm*. Every day from sunrise until sunset believers must go without food or drink. Many people also refrain from bad habits such as smoking, lying, using bad language, and getting angry, particularly during daylight hours. Everyone tries to

WORDS TO UNDERSTAND

Ablution: Washing of the body or hands; ritual bathing.
Date: The small brown fruit of the date palm, a common fruit in the Middle East and North Africa.
Iftar: The evening meal eaten after sunset during Ramadan.
Rakah: One unit of prayer in Islam, consisting of recitations of prayers and a series of bowing, kneeling, and prostrate postures.

◀ A Lebanese baker offers traditional cheese bread for a meal before sunrise during Ramadan, the holiest month for Muslims.

work together to avoid fighting and disagreements because getting angry at someone else is considered almost as bad as eating food during the fast. If a person cannot fast without health risks, then he or she is expected to give a specified amount to charity instead. The fast is meant to help Muslims cleanse their souls, concentrate on God, and improve their self-discipline. Fasting is also supposed to make believers more generous and sympathetic to the poor, who may not be able to afford food for themselves.

Children are not required to fast during Ramadan. Younger children may fast for part of a day or for a full day during the weekend, so that they too can participate in the ritual, but Muslims believe that nourishing growing bodies is more important than fasting. Usually people begin observing the full fast in their early teenage years.

Fasting is difficult, of course. Many Muslims turn to prayer and recitation of the Quran to help them. Long cycles of prayer and chanting of scripture help them take their minds off their stomachs.

■ Early to Rise

Because believers can eat only at night, most people get up very early in order to have a meal before the sun comes up. Throughout the Muslim world, women usually get up first to prepare the morning meal. This meal, called *suhur*, may take place as early as three in the morning, so many people try to eat quickly and then go right back to sleep. It is not smart to skip *suhur* because once the Sun comes up food and drink are off limits until darkness falls again.

SNACKING AFTER SUNSET

Many Muslims like to eat a date, a sweet brown fruit, as their first snack after sunset. The prophet Muhammad is said to have done this.

■ Evening Festivities

In the evenings, believers eagerly await the announcement from mosques or the media (television, radio, cell phone messages, and Web sites) that the sun has set. Many Muslims try to grab a quick snack as soon as this news arrives. A little later on they will eat a large meal known as **iftar**, which is often a feast. Many Muslims spend Ramadan visiting houses of family, friends, and neighbors every night to socialize and eat holiday treats. Cooks often prepare special foods that are particularly rich and sweet to make up for lost pleasures during the day.

After the *iftar* meal, Muslims may go out shopping. Shops and restaurants stay open late and groups of families and friends may stay out until 1 A.M. or later. They then wake up early again the next morning to eat before sunrise. In predominantly Muslim countries, the pace of life slows down during Ramadan. Because people go to bed late and get up early in order to fit in meals during the nighttime hours, they may be sleepy during the day. Many Muslims try to take naps during the day to make up for their decreased sleep. People who have jobs that require heavy labor might try to do their hardest work in the morning, when they are fresh from sleep and their morning meal.

Though fasting and losing sleep can be challenging, many Muslims look forward to Ramadan. They enjoy the heightened spirituality and fellowship, and they welcome the greater awareness of God and of the poor that they gain through the daily discipline. Many Muslims miss the purity of the holy month when Ramadan ends.

▲ During the month of Ramadan, a cannon is fired to announce sunset and the end of another day's fasting in Dubai, United Arab Emirates.

■ Celebrating Eid

When the new Moon reappears after the month of fasting, Ramadan comes to an end. The next day is called Eid al-Fitr (or Id ul-Fitr), which means "Festival of the Breaking of the Fast." On this day Muslims thank Allah for giving them the self-control to make it through the month of fasting and celebrate the unity of family and of the Muslim community.

Experience Eid al-Fitr celebrations in India.

On the morning of Eid al-Fitr, Muslims wake up early, wash, and dress in their best clothes. People who can afford them like to wear fancy new clothes for the holiday, but simply wearing clean clothing is enough. They eat a small breakfast to indicate that the fast of Ramadan is over. Most families then go to their mosque or to an open arena that has been consecrated for the occasion.

▲ A family in Malaysia celebrates Eid al-Fitr, which marks the end of Ramadan.

There the religious leaders lead prayers and preach sermons. At the end of the service the believers greet one another with a ritual phrase that shows they have forgiven one another's sins and are at peace. They may also greet one another with the phrase "Eid Mubarak," which means "Blessed Festival" in Arabic.

In much of the Muslim world, the rest of the day is taken up with food, visits, and entertainment. Many towns hold street fairs with rides and games. Families gather in each other's homes to enjoy feasts featuring special sweet food traditionally served on Eid al-Fitr, and adults give children gifts of money.

In many Muslim regions, people celebrate Eid al-Fitr for three days. Although the second two days are not actually religious holidays, most Muslims are happy to treat themselves to three (or more) days of constant feasting after the long days of fasting.

■ Overindulgence

Though some Muslims focus on prayers and fasting during Ramadan, others treat the season as a monthlong series of all-night parties. Weight gain during Ramadan is quite common, as people stuff themselves in the evenings after fasting all day. Doctors and religious leaders advise Muslims to eat carefully, but overindulgence is common. Religious leaders especially worry that the feasting is contrary to the spirit of Ramadan.

■ Prayer

Muslims are supposed to pray five times a day throughout the year. In Muslim cities and countries, religious leaders are the ones to call believers to prayer each time. These calls to prayer are especially important during Ramadan, when all believers have to coordinate both their prayers and their fasting. In previous centuries, religious

FOOD PRICES GO UP

Just as some toy prices may rise in the Western world as Christmas approaches, in the Islamic world, food costs more during Ramadan. Oddly, people actually buy more food than usual during Ramadan because they break the fast each day with special meals and prepare lavish feasts for Eid al-Fitr at the end of the month. A small fortune is spent on dates alone, as this fruit is a popular sunset snack. People also celebrate by buying presents, decorations for their homes, and new clothes for Eid al-Fitr. Just as in the Western world, Muslim families can put a strain on their finances at the holidays.

leaders called *muezzins* sang out calls to prayer from their mosques. Today, calls to prayer can be played over speakers or broadcast on television. Television stations also broadcast the start and end times of the fast each day and the schedule for prayer services in the mosques.

RITUALS OF RAMADAN PRAYER

During Ramadan Muslims bring a special focus to their prayers. Devout Muslims see the month as a special chance to put their spiritual affairs in order and bring themselves closer to Allah. Even Muslims who don't ordinarily pray daily may pray more during Ramadan.

Before prayers, Muslims wash their hands, mouths, noses, faces, and feet; their bodies, clothes, and prayer mats are supposed to be clean. Women must cover their hair. In fact, even women who do not ordinarily wear headscarves put them on for prayers, and many mosques require all women to cover their hair before entering. If a Muslim is praying at home or in some other area, he or she will lay a prayer mat on the floor or ground. Mosque floors are covered in thick, soft carpets for prayers.

ACHIEVING CLEANLINESS

Muslims can achieve cleanliness for prayers through three different types of bathing. Ordinarily before daily prayers they perform a partial **ablution**, or *wudu*, in which they wash the parts of the body exposed to dirt, such as hands, feet, and face. If for some reason a Muslim cannot wash with water, he or she can perform a "dry ablution," or dry bath, by touching clean sand or stone and then wiping both the hands and the face.

How much of their bodies women cover varies by society. In Tunisia, Indonesia, and Morocco women are not required to wear headscarves, though some do. In Turkey, many women wear no headscarves at all except when they attend services at the mosque, but devout women wear scarves that cover their hair completely. In Iran, women are expected to cover their heads and to wear long coats that cover their bodies, but they often wear form-fitting jeans underneath. In the United Arab Emirates, some women wear black robes that cover every part of their bodies except their eyes.

In Afghanistan, women are required to cover themselves head to foot in a garment called a *burqa*, which is like a giant sheet with a crocheted area over the face. Saudi Arabian women must wear a long black cloak that covers everything but their eyes. Religious police in these countries punish women who are caught uncovered.

▲ A four-year-old boy prepares to offer his prayers during Ramadan.

Hijab has long been a topic of debate among Muslims, and there are many different opinions on exactly what women must wear to be modest. During the 20th century, many Islamic countries loosened dress rules and women began dressing in Western clothing. In recent years, however, Islamic countries have become stricter and many women have gone back to wearing scarves and veils.

Muslims use their entire bodies when they pray. They stand, kneel, and place their heads on the floor. Each posture has a special meaning. Standing signifies that the person is ready to hear God and wants to obey him. Bowing down expresses humility and willingness to bow down to God's commands in everyday life.

◀ A man washes his hands before entering a mosque in Kashmir, India. Islam requires a ritual washing before prayer.

To begin prayers, Muslims face in the direction of Mecca, a city in Saudi Arabia that is the holiest place in Islam. They stand with their hands at their sides and recite a series of prayers in Arabic, periodically bowing. They also kneel, bending forward to touch their foreheads to the floor. Muslims go from standing to kneeling to bending to the ground several times during a set of prayers. Each set of ritual postures is called a **rakah**. Before beginning prayers, a Muslim will announce how many *rakah* he or she intends to perform. During Ramadan, devout Muslims will perform many more *rakah* than usual.

SPECIAL PRAYERS DURING RAMADAN

Many mosques hold nightly Ramadan prayers called *tarawih* that last one or two hours. Although not required, the *tarawih* offer a welcome social opportunity. In addition, many Muslims try to read the entire Quran during Ramadan. In some mosques, the religious leaders read portions of the Quran aloud every night, dividing the book into 30 sections so that they can finish the entire book during the month of Ramadan.

■ Charity

Just as in many other faiths, Muslims are expected to give a portion of their wealth to the mosque and to the poor. This contribution, called *zakat* or *zakah*, is generally expected to total 2 percent of a Muslim's wealth each year. Typically, believers bring their contributions to the mosque and in turn the money is distributed to the needy. Muslims often choose to pay the *zakat* during Ramadan, partly so that poor families can use the money to pay for their Eid celebrations at Ramadan's end.

THE RAMADAN EXPERIENCE FOR NON-MUSLIMS

Ramadan can be difficult for non-Muslims living in or visiting predominantly Islamic regions. Many businesses close or offer limited services because their workers are focused on fasting and praying (or taking a nap). Some restaurants close during the daytime so it can be hard for visitors to find food. (If someone is visiting an Islamic country during Ramadan, he or she should not eat or drink in front of people during the day or offer anyone food or drink. It is considered rude.) Traffic tends to snarl in the evenings as people rush home to be with their families by sunset. Many workers take the last week or two of Ramadan off from work, which slows business even more.

▲ Iraqis offer their prayers at a mosque during Ramadan in Baghdad, Iraq.

Many Muslim communities organize their own charitable drives during Ramadan to raise money for the poor in their local areas. A village or neighborhood might ask all households for donations of money or goods or hold fund-raising events such as concerts. Individual families try to do their part as well, perhaps inviting less fortunate families to eat *iftar* meals with them.

Ramadan is the highlight of the year for many Muslims around the world. They relish the chance to focus on their faith, family, and friends. Also, because most Muslims observe the ritual fasting, it reinforces a sense of community among Muslims of all backgrounds.

TEXT-DEPENDENT QUESTIONS

1: What is the most important practice of Ramadan?

2: When does Eid al-Fitr take place?

3: What is a *zakat?*

RESEARCH PROJECTS

1: Research some of the key artistic traditions of the Islamic world, including calligraphy, weaving, painting, and others. Write a brief report on one of these art forms, including its history in the Islamic world, notable works and practitioners, and other details.

2: Research the city of Mecca in Saudi Arabia. Find out about its history, location and geography, significance to Islam, and the pilgrimages of the Hajj and the Umrah. Write a brief report summarizing what you learned.

Observing in Africa

Although scholars do not know precisely how many Africans are Muslim, it is estimated that about 45 percent of the population practices the Islamic religion. North African nations are almost entirely Islamic. Islam is also quite common in western Africa, where about half the population is Muslim. Large numbers of Muslims also live in eastern Africa and central Africa. Muslims live in southern Africa too, although they are a small minority.

WORDS TO UNDERSTAND

Baklava: Pastries made of phyllo dough, chopped nuts, butter, and honey that are popular throughout the Middle East and eastern Mediterranean region.
Circumcision: The act of cutting the foreskin from a boy's or man's penis, commonly done as an act of initiation in Judaism and Islam.
Couscous: A type of granular pasta made by forming the dough of semolina flour into tiny grains, commonly eaten with soup, vegetables, and meat.

◀ A man sells religious reading outside a mosque in Uganda.

■ Ramadan in Africa

North African Ramadan practices are similar to those in the Middle East. South of the Sahara Desert, however, Islam is practiced in slightly different ways, influenced by local cultural traditions and languages.

In North Africa, many people start praying and fasting ahead of Ramadan to get in shape spiritually. During Ramadan, mosques are packed with men praying the five daily prayers. Women also go to mosques to pray; in many mosques, women pray upstairs while men pray downstairs. Children accompany their parents to the mosques and spend prayer time playing outside on the grass. After evening prayers, many people like to recite the Quran.

In African nations with large Islamic populations, Ramadan dictates daily schedules. In countries with a smaller Islamic presence, Muslims must fit their religious observance into their daily routine.

NAPPING IN THE MOSQUE

After noon prayers, many men in Africa take advantage of the soft carpeted floor and cool air of the mosque to take a quick nap.

In Tunisia, Libya, and other Islamic nations life changes during Ramadan. Everyone, Muslim and non-Muslim alike, puts off social engagements such as parties and weddings until the month is over. National television and radio stations devote almost all of their programming to Muslim topics, such as sermons or quizzes on theology. Buses, trains, post offices, and businesses may adopt different hours of operation.

In Islamic regions, Ramadan is also a time of shopping. Many shops and food vendors are closed during morning hours but open around 1 P.M. so that people can do their shopping for the evening meal. Afternoon markets in Tunisia, Algeria, and other areas are full of people purchasing food to break their fasts. Certain items such as dates, **couscous**, and oil become much more expensive during Ramadan because everyone needs them to prepare traditional delicacies. Food merchants enjoy Ramadan because they have many customers and can charge them high prices.

In the early evening, African Muslims desert the streets to await the announcement of sunset. In many places, this event is announced by the firing of a cannon although some families get the news over the radio or television instead. After the sun sets, everyone eats a meal and says evening prayers. In Africa, Muslims put a great deal of energy into preparing food for Ramadan evening meals and for Eid al-Fitr celebrations at month's end. Popular Tunisian foods during

▲ A Nigerian Muslim washes before attending noon prayers at a mosque in Lagos, Nigeria.

Ramadan include flat breads, Turkish delight (a fruit-flavored gelatin candy), cakes, cookies, dates, couscous, meat pastries, soup, fresh salads, fresh fruits, and fresh lemon juice.

In some North African nations, many restaurants and cafés close once the fast has been broken and the evening meal consumed. At this time people living in cities in Tunisia, Libya, Algeria, or other population centers head back out into the streets. Shops open again and are crammed with people amusing themselves by chatting, drinking coffee, and buying desserts from pastry shops.

In small North African towns, after *iftar* people often relax by watching television or reading. People might gather at a local shop or café to talk to friends and drink coffee or mint tea. Often people take care of business during the evening hours and may stay up

SNEAKING MEALS AT OPEN RESTAURANTS

In Tunisia and other North African nations, many restaurants and cafés close during the day and open after sunset; but not all do—some Muslims are known to sneak a meal during the day.

much of the night shopping or working. After finishing the evening festivities, people head home to get some sleep before rising again for the day's work.

Some workers in North Africa take vacation during Ramadan so they can sleep late in the mornings. Others go to work very early, just after their dawn meals, and then sleep in the afternoons. Broken sleep and lack of food can make many people irritable for the entire month, but a festive atmosphere still pervades cities and towns.

STAYING UP LATE

Teenage boys who like to stay up all night often get to during Ramadan—and get to say that they're doing their religious duty!

In many areas, young men travel through neighborhoods playing drums to wake Muslims so that they have time to eat a quick meal before sunrise. In areas with smaller concentrations of Muslims, Ramadan happens more quietly. Still, Muslims often live together in Muslim neighborhoods where they can pray, fast, and celebrate as a community.

▲ Needy Muslims are served free rice and meat to break the fast in the evening during Ramadan at a mosque in Cairo, Egypt.

Eid al-Fitr in Africa

Eid al-Fitr is a major celebration for many African Muslims. The faithful put on their best new clothes and visit friends and relatives. Mothers in North African nations buy new clothes for their children for Eid al-Fitr, competing to have the best-dressed children. In Tunisia, small girls often wear frilly dresses with ribbons in their hair. Boys shoot toy guns and set off small firecrackers. Food and toy vendors set up stalls on the streets and children use the gifts of money they have just received to buy presents for themselves while their parents sit at sidewalk cafés. Many shops and businesses close for Eid al-Fitr and several days afterward, causing problems for people who forget to stock up on food before the holiday.

Eid al-Fitr can last for several days in Islamic nations. Moroccans, for example, celebrate Eid al-Fitr for three days. If the holiday falls in the middle of a week, businesses and schools may take the entire week off.

Unique Customs and Traditions

COMING OF AGE IN ALGERIA

In the weeks leading up to Ramadan, Algerian women devote themselves to cleaning and refurbishing their houses to get them ready for guests. They may buy new pots and pans, paint the walls, and wash the carpets. They also help clean the mosques.

Enjoy a Ramadan meal in Algeria.

Many women in Algeria also start buying food supplies for the month weeks ahead of time. Traditional Ramadan dishes include a soup made of lentils, tomatoes, chickpeas, onions, rice, eggs, and olive oil called *al-harira*; homemade bread called *al-kasra*; a bread filled with meat and cheese called *al-buraq*; almonds; **baklava**; and a honeyed doughnut called *zalabiya*. In contrast, Algeria's Ahaggar people, a group of Tuareg nomads, use Ramadan as a time to practice austerity, or simplicity, in cooking and to remind themselves of their traditional way of life. They eat plain foods, including dried dates, a vegetable soup called *hsa*, and tea. At this time the Algerian government distributes food packages to the needy. It also operates soup kitchens that serve meals to the homeless and to travelers during Ramadan.

During Ramadan Algerian boys who are coming of age have their heads shaved completely. They undergo their **circumcision** (cutting away of the male foreskin) during the last 10 days of

A TIME FOR SOCIAL EVENTS IN MALI

Unlike Muslims in other African countries, who put off social engagements until the month is over, Muslims in Mali like to hold weddings and other social events during Ramadan. At the end of the month, villages often celebrate the holiday with singing and dancing.

Ramadan, which is considered the holiest time for this event. A child who fasts during Ramadan for the first time receives a special present at its end, on Eid al-Fitr. His or her parents will place a gold or silver ring inside a sweet drink to signify that the child has begun to assume adult religious responsibilities.

TRADITIONAL DRESS IN ETHIOPIA

About one-third of Ethiopia's population is Muslim. On Eid al-Fitr, many of these Muslims gather at stadiums and open-air arenas to listen to religious leaders. People dress in traditional Ethiopian attire and wave the Ethiopian flag. In 2007, a number of Christian religious leaders also attended Eid al-Fitr gatherings to emphasize the need for Ethiopia's diverse people to live in harmony and religious tolerance.

MUSLIMS READ THE QURAN IN MALAWI

Muslims make up about 12 percent of Malawi's population. The poorer Muslims of Malawi spend the weeks before Ramadan stockpiling enough food to get them through the month of evening feasts. They try to acquire and save food before Ramadan begins to avoid having to depend on handouts from the rich. Once Ramadan starts, food prices go up, sometimes more than doubling in Malawi. Popular Ramadan foods include rice (the most important staple food in Malawi) along with potatoes, sweet potatoes, and cassava, a starchy root vegetable.

Like Muslims elsewhere, the Muslims in Malawi like to spend Ramadan studying the Quran. In the past this was difficult for many of them because they did not read Arabic, but in 2006, Malawians received copies of the Quran in their local language, Chichewa, as a gift from King Fahd of Saudi Arabia. In addition, the Muslim Association of Malawi offers lectures to workers to tell them how to take the message of Ramadan into the workplace. In particular, religious leaders instruct workers that they must not shirk their duties simply because they are fasting.

◀ A father and son, wearing new clothes for the occasion, walk to an Eid al-Fitr celebration in Addis Ababa, Ethiopia. The festival of Eid al-Fitr marks the end of the monthlong fast of Ramadan.

STAYING UP ALL NIGHT IN MOROCCO

In Morocco, people may adapt their work schedules to fit Ramadan's requirements. They may not go to sleep at all during the night, staying up from *iftar* until sunrise chatting and praying. In the early morning, they work for a while before going home to sleep until sunset.

In small towns in Morocco, the evening meal can be fairly simple. Moroccans often break a day's fast with a lentil soup called *harira*, which can be served hot or cold, depending on the season. Then a family may eat a meal of fish or meat and vegetables, sometimes with couscous, a type of cooked granular pasta.

MUSICIANS PLAY RAMADAN MUSIC IN NIGERIA

During Ramadan in Nigeria, mosques are crammed with believers who come to daily prayers or *tarawih* prayers at night. Because many Nigerian Muslims do not speak Arabic, the language of the Quran, Nigerian mosques have begun offering recitations of the Quran translated into local languages such as Yoruba, Hausa, and Igbo in order to reach all believers.

Some local governments offer afternoon sessions of *tafseer*, or commentary on the Quran. Governments also serve evening *iftar* meals to guests. Islamic organizations offer a number of educational lectures before and during Ramadan, in which experts teach listeners about Islamic law, Muslim rights, and the reasons to fast during Ramadan.

◀ Two Muslim boys take a break while reading the Quran at a mosque in Cape Town, South Africa during Ramadan.

In southwest Nigeria there are groups of musicians that specialize in a type of music called *ejisaari*, which means "wake up for *suhur*" in the Yoruba language. Because people eat *suhur* at about 2 A.M., these musicians begin playing in the middle of the night. They carry drums and sing, moving from house to house and calling to specific inhabitants to wake up and say their prayers.

▲ Dried dates for sale at an Algerian bazaar. The sweet fruits are a popular food to break the fast at sunset.

Families pay them with gifts of food, clothing, or money. This service is especially valuable in more remote towns and villages that may not have electricity or radio reception. These musical groups also compete in national contests to determine the best Muslim musicians in Nigeria.

UNSAFE RAMADAN IN SOMALIA

Somalia has been in a state of violence and civil unrest since 1991, which has made it nearly impossible for Somalis to observe Ramadan. There are few charities left in the country, food supplies have been low, and in many areas it is unsafe for people to leave their homes. In 2006, however, Somali Muslims did get to celebrate Ramadan after the government defeated the warlords who were ravaging the country. Families once again enjoyed shopping at the marketplace and admiring the decorations in the streets. Nevertheless, conditions are still uncertain and the Muslims of Somalia are not likely to enjoy regular and safe Ramadan celebrations for some time.

MUSLIMS OF INDIAN DESCENT IN SOUTH AFRICA

There are more than 500 mosques in South Africa and numerous Muslim schools. Most of South Africa's Muslims are descendants of people who emigrated from India. They still like to eat Indian foods. Months before Ramadan begins, family cooks begin preparing delicacies for Ramadan evening meals. Popular foods include Indian-style curries, *samosas*, and a soup called *haleem*.

All major South African cities have Islamic radio stations. During Ramadan, South Africa's mosques are crowded with worshippers who come in the evenings to say *tarawih* prayers; women may stay home to perform *tarawih* on their own. Muslims often give up movies and other entertainment in favor of reciting the Quran during Ramadan. People visit the graves of their relatives and say prayers for the dead. Some Muslims choose to spend the day visiting the sick in hospitals or orphans.

HOSPITALITY IN SUDAN

After a morning of fasting, the open-air markets in Sudan's capital city, Khartoum, become crammed in the afternoon with shoppers bargaining with merchants to get the best price on fruits and vegetables for the evening meal. One popular food in Sudan is *roegag*, a cereal made of wheat flour and milk. A popular drink is *abreh*, which is made from sorghum (syrup from the juice of a sorgo plant that resembles cane syrup). Sudanese families eat sitting on the ground, often outside their houses. They spread mats on the ground and place the food on them. When people walk by, they are invited to join the meal, and it is impolite to decline such an invitation. This hospitality strengthens relationships between neighbors and also allows families to provide charity to those who might be on the road, unable to get to their own homes to break the fast. Sudan has many poor people. In addition to invitations from people in the community, they are helped during Ramadan by charitable organizations. Aid agencies organize large *iftar* meals for those who cannot prepare their own and follow the meals with lessons on the Quran. Volunteers stand on the roads at the day's end and offer dates and water to people who cannot make it home by sunset.

 ## TEXT-DEPENDENT QUESTIONS

1: What are some popular Tunisian foods during Ramadan?

2: What are the ingredients of *al-harira*?

3: Where is the city of Khartoum?

 ## RESEARCH PROJECTS

1: Find recipes for some of the traditional Ramadan dishes mentioned in this chapter. Compare and contrast different recipes from region to region, noting differences in ingredients, spices, or other components. Create a short "Ramadan cookbook" incorporating these different recipes and any additional information you might have found.

2: Research the Salah times, or hours of prayer in the Muslim world. Create an outline of these prayer times, including their official name, when they occur, how long they last, and what they mean. If possible, include details about specific prayer rituals such as movements and gestures.

Observing in Asia

About 40 percent of the population of Southeast Asia is Muslim. Islam is the official religion in Malaysia and Brunei, and one of the official religions of Indonesia. Islam is also the most common religion in Bangladesh, Pakistan, Afghanistan, and the Central Asian nations of Kazakhstan, Turkmenistan, Uzbekistan, and Kyrgyzstan. More than 82 percent of the population of Central Asia is Muslim. Muslims also live in other Asian nations, including China, India, and Mongolia.

■ Ramadan in Asia

Observance of Ramadan varies throughout the region. In heavily Islamic areas, such as Indonesia and Malaysia, Ramadan can completely transform daily life as everyone adopts the schedule of early rising and daily fasting. In other areas, Ramadan is not as

WORDS TO UNDERSTAND

Henna: Designs made with the reddish-brown dye from the leaves of a henna plant.
Seviyan: A pudding made of vermicelli and milk, popular in India and Pakistan.
Somber: Dull or dark in tone.

◀ A Bangladeshi street vendor sells traditional fast-breaking foods for Ramadan.

obvious. In western China and the Central Asian republics, for example, many years of government suppression of religion have resulted in a decline in the number of practicing Muslims and thus the public observance of Islamic traditions.

Muslims throughout Asia consider Ramadan the most important month of the religious calendar. They fast, pray, and try to improve themselves. Ramadan is not all serious, however. Muslims in Asia also spend the month feasting, shopping, and visiting friends and relatives.

Asian Muslims make a special effort during Ramadan to perform their five daily prayers. Huge numbers of believers gather at mosques throughout Asia, where some people like to recite the Quran together. Worshippers in large cities, such as Delhi, India, might even spill out the doors of the mosque into the courtyard.

BREAKING THE FAST WITH REGIONAL FOODS

Favorite foods for breaking the fast vary by region. In Southeast Asia, dates are a popular sweet snack for breaking the fast. On Eid al-Fitr, many Asians eat a dish called *sivvayan* or *seviyan*, a sweet pudding made of vermicelli noodles. This is popular in Pakistan, Bangladesh, and India.

At the end of a day during Ramadan, believers listen for the signal that the Sun has set and that they can break their fast. This signal might be a call to prayer from a mosque. It might also be broadcast on television or the radio. As soon as believers hear that the fast is over for the day, they eat a quick snack. In Southeast Asia this snack often consists of sweet tidbits, especially the dates that are popular throughout the Islamic world, and a very sweet drink. After the snack, believers perform their evening prayers. They often go to the mosque for this. Evening prayers can be an enjoyable social event, with friends and neighbors gathering to celebrate their faith.

The evening meal during Ramadan is a festive occasion. Women throughout the Islamic world spend much of the day cooking for meals at home in the evening. In Jakarta, the capital of Indonesia, Kuala Lumpur, the capital of Malaysia, and other major Islamic cities, restaurants often open special buffets in the evenings, which can become packed with diners breaking their fast.

Businesses in Indonesia might adjust their décor to reflect the season; for example, restaurants might cover up nude statues or paintings. Many businesses cut back on their hours or close down entirely. Some restaurants close during the day. Others, particularly those in larger cities stay open to serve daytime meals to non-Muslims but they may close their curtains so that fasting Muslims who walk by do not have to watch people eating.

Muslims who are fasting usually wake up before dawn in order to have a meal before the Sun comes up. In Southeast Asia and other largely Islamic areas, the mosques will broadcast a call to prayer over a loudspeaker. As in Africa, boys in Southeast Asia march through the streets banging on drums to awaken sleepers. Young Muslims can be quite enthusiastic about this job, which allows them to walk around the town in the dark making a lot of noise. This early rising gives people plenty of time to make and eat the pre-dawn meal.

In Southeast Asia, neighborhoods organize charitable drives to collect money and goods for the poor people in the area. During the last 10 days of Ramadan, beggars from the countryside swarm into big cities hoping to collect alms. They gather at traffic lights and ask passing motorists for gifts of money.

■ Eid al-Fitr in Asia

The days leading up to Eid al-Fitr are some of the busiest in Asia. Devout Muslims perform extra prayers and make a special effort to read the Quran even more. In Southeast Asia, Eid al-Fitr is also used as an occasion for people to make formal apologies and requests for forgiveness.

In addition to these extra prayers and apologies, Southeast Asian Muslims gear up to do their shopping and family activities. Women start cooking foods for the feast on Eid al-Fitr, beginning their preparations two weeks or so before the end of Ramadan. The day of Eid al-Fitr is a huge occasion throughout most of Islamic Asia. People once again wake before dawn. They bathe and dress in new clothes if they have them; if not, they at least dress in clean clothing. They eat a small snack to show that the fast is over, and then they attend prayers. Many people go to a mosque. Others attend large services in open spaces such as courtyards or stadiums, which have been consecrated by religious leaders for the occasion.

The rest of the day is devoted to feasting and merrymaking. People visit one another and eat special foods. Older people give money to children. In India and Pakistan, many people go shopping or go out to eat.

■ Unique Customs and Traditions

CELEBRATION IN AFGHANISTAN

In Afghanistan, many people do not have electricity, so they eat their pre-dawn breakfast and drink cups of tea by the light of candles or kerosene lamps. During Ramadan, Afghan men visit the barber to have their beards trimmed. Afghans celebrate Eid al-Fitr for three days. On the first day, anyone who has had a death in the family during the year is supposed to stay home and receive visitors

FESTIVE GARB

Malaysians wear colorful traditional clothing for Eid al-Fitr, in stark contrast to the somber black and gray Islamic attire of countries such as Afghanistan or Saudi Arabia.

coming to pay their respects. A host is careful to provide enough dried fruits, sweets, and hot tea for all the guests.

THE NIGHT OF POWER IN BANGLADESH

Bangladesh's population is 83 percent Muslim. In Bangladesh, the 27th day of Ramadan, called Shab e-Qadr, the "night of power," is an especially important holiday. Muslims believe that if they pray through this night, all their sins will be forgiven. Bangladeshi Muslims take this day very seriously. Muslim men gather at mosques while women stay at home to pray. The men say the Isha prayer at sunset and then keep praying until midnight. The next day is a national holiday. Bangladeshi newspapers and magazines publish special articles about Shab e-Qadr and television and radio stations broadcast programs that highlight the importance of the holiday.

▲ Muslims in Selangor, Malaysia performing Zakat, an act of charity required during Ramadan. Those who can afford to are expected to donate money and clothing to the poor.

MUSLIMS IN CHINA

About 21 million Muslims live in China. About 7.5 million of them are members of the Uighur ("wee-gur") group in Xinjiang, a region in northwestern China. The Chinese government does not allow these Muslims to take breaks from their regular school or work routine to observe Ramadan. Schoolchildren and state employees are sometimes required to eat lunch during fasting days. They are not always given time to go to mosques to pray during the day and in some areas people are not allowed to stay in the mosques at night. Muslims in other parts of China often do not keep up Muslim practices such as fasting. Nevertheless, China's Muslims still engage in large celebrations and prayers during Ramadan, particularly in Xinjiang. Although the government does not recognize Ramadan, Eid-al-Fitr is an official holiday in some predominantly Muslim parts of China, and even non-Muslim Chinese people celebrate it.

NIGHT OF THE MOON IN INDIA

In India's Muslim communities, people spend the last few days of Ramadan preparing for Eid al-Fitr. The last night of Ramadan is called Chand Raat, which means "night of the Moon." Entire families

▲ People wash themselves with water in New Delhi, India as they prepare for Iftar—the evening meal to break the sunrise to sunset fast.

spend this evening shopping at malls and bazaars. Young women and girls dress up in colorful clothing, wear a lot of jewelry, and paint **henna** designs (designs made with the reddish-brown dye from the leaves of a henna plant) on their hands. The next morning they go out to visit friends and family, greeting each other with the words "Eid Mubarak," which means "blessed festival." Older people often give children gifts of money.

VISITING GRAVES IN INDONESIA

In Indonesia and other Islamic areas of Southeast Asia, devout Muslims visit the graves of deceased family members the day before Ramadan begins. This custom is not typical of Muslim practices in other areas, and Islamic purists say that the practice is un-Islamic. For many Asian people, however, honoring dead ancestors is very important, so they have incorporated this tradition into their religious practices.

Many Muslims in Indonesia take the last 10 days or so of Ramadan as holidays from work. Much of the population travels to visit their families. During Eid al-Fitr in Indonesia, young people ask older family members for forgiveness. A child or young person kneels in front of the older person, bows his or her head to the elder's knees, and asks for forgiveness. Because so many travel to their hometowns, the population of Indonesia's capital, Jakarta, usually decreases by one-third. It is difficult to buy airplane, train, or bus tickets at this time because most Muslims who live in cities book them in order to visit their families. Buses and trains become incredibly crowded, and highways are jammed with cars.

HOSPITALITY IN KAZAKHSTAN

In Kazakhstan, people celebrate Eid al-Fitr by visiting friends and relatives. Hospitality is very important to Kazakhs. Every host offers refreshments to visitors and is offended if they do not accept something. Some Kazakhs live in traditional *yurts*, or large tents, though others live in apartments. When visitors come, they first wash their hands and then come inside to say a prayer. They then eat foods, which might include dried or fresh fruits, mutton (sheep meat), soup, and tea or *kymyz*, a drink made from horse milk. One special treat on Eid al-Fitr is deep-fried doughnuts called *baursaki*. In Kazakhstan, adults eat first; children can eat what is left over after the adults are done.

DAY OF CELEBRATION IN MALAYSIA

In Malaysia, food vendors set up special booths during Ramadan selling local delicacies that people buy and bring home for the evening meal to save themselves the trouble of cooking. People often break their fast with *satay* (pieces of meat cooked on a wooden skewer and dipped in peanut sauce), fish curry, rice cooked in coconut milk, fish, and tropical fruit.

▲ Indonesian Muslim women pray during the start of celebrations for the Eid al-Fitr holiday.

▲ A street vendor in Malaysia prepares food for the traditional fast-breaking meal during Ramadan.

Malaysian religious officials spend the last night of Ramadan watching the Moon from hilltops throughout the country. Once they see the new Moon, Ramadan ends

Observe Ramadan preparations in Pakistan.

and Eid al-Fitr begins. In Malaysia, Eid al-Fitr is called Hari Raya, which means "Day of Celebration." It is the biggest celebration of the Ramadan season. During the last 10 days of Ramadan, shopping centers are clogged with people buying supplies for the festival. Malaysians observe the first two days of this month as a public holiday, but many of them take a whole week off, sometimes traveling long distances to spend the holiday with their family and friends. On the first day after Ramadan, Muslims dress in new clothes for prayers at the mosque; many people choose traditional Malaysian garments for this special occasion. They then eat breakfast at home with their families. During the rest of the day they visit and clean the graves of dead family members and visit friends and relatives. This is also the day for people to apologize to anyone they may have hurt during the previous year. The traditional greeting that people exchange on Eid al-Fitr, "maaf zahirdan batin," means "forgive me for all my sins."

▲ The whole family gathers to ask forgiveness from their elders on Eid Al-Fitr, called Hari Raya in Malaysia.

FESTIVAL OF SWEETS IN PAKISTAN

After sunset during Ramadan, Pakistanis often first eat a date and then follow it with a bowl of *chaat*, a mixture of many kinds of fruits. Another popular Ramadan dish is deep-fried vermicelli noodles, called *khajlaphehni*. In Pakistan, people call the end of Ramadan the "festival of sweets." After spending a month fasting, people take advantage of Eid al-Fitr to eat all the sweet foods they denied themselves during Ramadan. On the morning of Eid al-Fitr, Muslims dress in new clothes and go to the mosque to pray. They then begin attending the many parties that are held that day. Every host offers an assortment of good foods to eat: chai, a spicy black tea with milk and sugar; flat breads called *naan* and *pooris*; pink cakes called *chum chum*; a warm rice pudding called *kheer*; *jalebis*, fried sugar candies shaped like pretzels; cakes called *mithai*; cheese cakes called *kalakand*; and a traditional dish of sweetened fried vermicelli noodles called *seviyan*.

 ## TEXT-DEPENDENT QUESTIONS

1: What type of noodles are in *seviyan*?

2: What is the name for the last night of Ramadan, and what does it mean?

3: What is Eid al-Fitr called in Malaysia?

 ## RESEARCH PROJECTS

1: Research the history, culture, language, and religion of the Uighur people of Central Asia. Write a brief summary of your findings, including information about the recent struggles between the Uighur and the Chinese government.

2: Research Sufism, the mystical tradition of Islam. Write a brief report including information about its origins, teachings, notable Sufis throughout history, literary works, and other spiritual and cultural contributions.

Observing in Europe

5

everal million Muslims live in Europe. Some of them live in neighborhoods that are predominantly Islamic and have managed to preserve much of their culture from home. Others live in areas where they are in a small minority. In either case, Muslims living in Europe face the challenge of celebrating Ramadan in countries that do not observe the month as a national holiday.

■ Ramadan in Europe

For those who remember Ramadan in the Islamic countries of their birth, the smaller European version of the holiday may be disappointing. But for Muslim children born in Europe, this Ramadan is all they know, and they look forward to it just as their neighbors and classmates may anticipate Christmas or Hanukkah.

Fitting the ritual practices of Ramadan into European daily life can be difficult. The early rising and unusual meal times sometimes clash with **secular** schedules.

WORDS TO UNDERSTAND

Communism: A political system in which all property is publicly owned.
Protectorate: A state that is protected and controlled by another state.
Secular: Not affiliated with religion or spirituality.

◀ German men and women share a meal with Muslim refugees to break the fast during Ramadan.

PRAYING IN CASTLES AND PALACES

In 2006, Queen Elizabeth of the United Kingdom gave permission for a room to be set aside in Windsor Castle for Muslims to pray in during Ramadan. Buckingham Palace already had a designated Ramadan prayer area.

In France, for example, Muslim students sometimes fall asleep in school after getting up early to eat breakfast and pray. Many European countries do try to accommodate Ramadan, however, to make it easier for their Muslim inhabitants. Many companies try to help Muslim employees fast by postponing parties until after Ramadan, when Muslims can join the fun.

Some European Muslims try to avoid being around people who are eating and drinking during the day because it makes fasting more difficult. They miss the feeling of sharing Ramadan with an entire community. Others, particularly secular Muslims who do not observe all Islamic traditions, feel the opposite way. They like the fact that in non-Muslim countries fasting is a matter of personal choice and they do not feel the social pressure to fast that they would feel in Muslim nations. One challenge of practicing Islam in Europe is that there are no loud announcements or cannon shots in the evening to publicize that the Sun has set. European Muslims must be resourceful to find out when they must begin and end Ramadan and when they can break their fasts.

■ Eid al-Fitr in Europe

As in other Muslim communities, Eid al-Fitr in Europe is observed with prayers, feasts, and celebrations among family and friends. In the days before Eid al-Fitr, women shop for new clothes and foods for cooking a festive Eid al-Fitr breakfast. After gathering at mosques for morning services, people get together to listen to Islamic music, exchange gifts, and rejoice in the feelings of peace and goodwill that follow the holy month of Ramadan.

■ Unique Customs and Traditions

RAMADAN IN POST-COMMUNIST BOSNIA AND HERZEGOVINA

Bosnia and Herzegovina historically has a large Muslim population and, in the past, Ramadan and Eid al-Fitr were major celebrations. Muslims would say prayers together during the day and then invite one another to their homes for *iftar* meals. It was considered an honor to host an imam, a religious leader, in one's home. People would make their own meals from food they raised. They would eat pastries filled with potatoes, cheese, meat, or spinach.

Experience scenes of Ramadan in Bosnia and Herzegovina.

They also ate a dish called *topa*, which combined cheese, butter, and cream, and Turkish pastries such as baklava.

In pre-communist Bosnia, on Eid al-Fitr, which was called Bairam, people would walk from village to village to greet one another. During the day, the people engaged in singing, dancing, and games. Winners of athletic contests would receive prizes of hand-made clothing. This was also considered the best day on which to circumcise boys.

Communism, however, repressed most of the Muslim folk traditions in Bosnia between 1945 and 1992. Yugoslavia's communist government, under leader Josip Broz Tito, suppressed all

▲ A Bosnian Muslim woman prays at a mosque during Ramadan in Sarajevo, the capital of Bosnia and Herzegovina.

types of religion. Political leaders were not allowed to attend religious services. The government closed down religious schools. Parents might secretly teach their children about their faith, but any sense of religious community disappeared over the years. Ethnic violence directed at Muslims during the war of the 1990s did nothing to restore Muslim culture.

FEEDING THE POOR

British Muslims who cannot fast for health reasons are supposed to feed a poor person for each day of fasting that they miss by paying money to a local mosque. In England in 2017, the going rate for a missed fast was £7.60 (British pounds) a day.

Today, many urban Muslims in Bosnia and Herzegovina do not feel a strong sense of community. Families might celebrate Ramadan and Eid al-Fitr privately, but they do not feel comfortable visiting or hosting their neighbors the way people used to. Only a few decades ago the people of this region were killing one another because of religion, and it will take some time for them to trust one another again. However, it is possible that Muslim traditions will come back. People who live in the country, especially in areas with majority Muslim populations, are more likely to observe religious traditions. In addition, young people of all religions are more likely to be religious than their parents now that religious freedom is possible again.

MUSLIMS TURN ON THE RADIO IN ENGLAND

About 2.8 million Muslims live in the United Kingdom, the majority of which are concentrated in London. Most British Muslims are Sunnis from Pakistan, Bangladesh, and India. For many British Muslims, Ramadan is a private affair, shared with family members and Islamic friends. Cities are not decorated for the holiday as they are in Muslim nations, but families may decorate their own houses. Children make Ramadan cards or collect pennies for the poor in donation boxes.

Some British radio stations broadcast special programs during Ramadan. Religious experts will speak about Ramadan in Urdu, the language spoken by many Pakistani immigrants, or in other languages, depending on the composition of the audience. Listeners can call the radio station to ask questions of the expert. The stations also broadcast recitations of the Quran and sermons, as well as calls to prayer. A Web site also announces calls to prayer. Some people sign up for daily text messages on their cell phones to tell them when to pray. Others form their own prayer "alert networks," groups of friends who call one another just before prayer times. These alerts take the place of the calls to prayer that are common in Muslim nations but are illegal or nonexistent in

England. (Muslim calls to prayer are loud announcements broadcast several times a day, including in the wee hours of the morning; many towns have laws against this type of loud noise.) Modern Muslims can even use GPS to find the direction of Mecca so that they will know which direction to face as they pray.

British Muslims often eat aromatic basmati brown rice (the same type of rice eaten in Pakistan), hummus (a blended chickpea spread), stuffed grape leaves, and kebabs. Some Muslims add traditional English foods such as Yorkshire pudding to their *iftar* meals. For Ramadan breakfasts, many British Muslims choose to eat English oatmeal because it keeps them full for a long time.

One challenge faced by British Muslims is becoming aware of when Eid al-Fitr will fall. Eid is not a national holiday in the United Kingdom, so people must ask permission to take the day off from work. Because different groups of Muslims celebrate Eid at different times, and because the exact date is not known until the new Moon is sighted anyway, there is always the chance of getting the day wrong. In that case, employees sometimes must quickly call their jobs and try to get a different day off.

FAMOUS FOR PASTRIES IN FRANCE

Somewhere between 4 and 6 million Muslims are estimated to live in France, or from 3 to 10 percent of the population. Many of these Muslims come from France's former colonies and **protectorates** in North Africa, especially Algeria, Morocco, and Tunisia. France's culture is generally secular, meaning the government does not advocate or promote any particular religion and has passed some laws limiting religious expression in public.

As Ramadan approaches, Muslim bakeries and butcher shops in France begin preparing special foods that Muslims will want to buy during the month of fasting. Algerian bakeries sell pastries called *zlabia*. Moroccan food shops set up tables covered with breads and pastries for Ramadan meals. Even non-Muslim grocery stores stock extra dates for the season.

CONTROVERSY IN FRANCE

In 2004 France passed a law that students and teachers in French schools are not allowed to wear conspicuous religious symbols such as the headscarves worn by many Muslim girls and women. Some of France's Muslims like the secular nature of French society and do not mind that they cannot show their religion publicly. Others find the idea of going out in public without their traditional Islamic coverings unacceptable.

Most French towns and workplaces accommodate Ramadan practices. French Muslims get up before dawn to eat a quick meal and pray before the Sun rises. Many believers go to mosques to say their daily prayers. After the Sun sets, Muslims break their fast together. A number of Muslims eat their evening meal in mosques, several of which offer traditional North African food such as couscous and lentil *harira* soup. Religious leaders preach evening sermons, often speaking in both French and Arabic.

Many French families check the newspaper or radio to find out exactly what time the Sun sets. Muslim radio stations announce the event as it happens. French Muslims eat different snacks as their first food; some start with soup, while others eat the traditional dates washed down with mint tea. After this snack and evening prayers, people eat a large evening meal. They may eat flat breads, boiled eggs, pastries stuffed with meat or fish, lentil *harira* soup, lamb, and pastries.

ELECTRONIC GOOD WISHES IN GERMANY

As of 2010, there were about 4.8 million Muslims living in Germany. Most are of Turkish origin, the families and descendants of people who came from Turkey to work in the mid-1900s. Germany is home to large groups of Muslims, many of whom live in Muslim enclaves within the cities. Germany's capital city Berlin, for example, has large Islamic areas.

German bakeries stock up on the special foods Muslims eat during Ramadan. These include dates, a licorice-flavored drink called *suus*, date syrup called *dschellab*, and a juice made from dried apricots called *qamruddin*. Bakeries sell Ramadan pastries that are not available for most of the year. Some groceries with large Muslim clienteles import fruits, vegetables, and other foods from the Middle East.

In the Islamic areas of German cities and towns, many people gather for *iftar* meals; the deserted streets in the evenings are said to resemble those of Istanbul, the largest city in Turkey at that time of day. German Muslims sometimes invite non-Muslim neighbors to *iftar*. They want to show their friends and neighbors what Ramadan is like and to share the festive spirit of Ramadan with non-Muslims. Many Muslims in Europe worry about the reputation that Islam has in the world, and hope that sharing Ramadan hospitality can dispel people's beliefs about Islam being a religion of extremists.

On Eid al-Fitr, Germany's mosques overflow with worshippers. After services, Muslims hold family gatherings where they feast to celebrate the end of fasting. Parents and other adults give children presents, such as new clothes, candy, or toys. Many Muslims living in Germany also send a flurry of messages to friends and relatives living far and near. They use modern technology, sending text messages, e-mails, e-cards, and faxes with good wishes for the holiday.

▲ Muslim men attend a special Ramadan prayer service in Berlin, Germany.

◀ A Muslim man in Germany performs ritual washing before entering the mosque to pray during Ramadan.

THE GROWTH OF ISLAM IN ITALY

About 1.6 million Muslims live in Italy. They come from many different countries and regions, including Tunisia, Algeria, Egypt, Morocco, Senegal, Turkey, Southeast Asia, and the Balkan nations. Many Muslims living in Italy are guest workers who do not live with their families. They often go to the several mosques in Italy that hold communal *iftar* banquets in the evenings so that if they cannot be with family they can at least be with their religious communities. In cities with substantial Muslim populations, it is common to see men going to prayers at mosques and women doing their shopping in headscarves and veils. There are nine mosques in Italy's capital, Rome. In Milan, Italy's second-largest city, there are four Islamic centers, however; they are not large enough to hold all the worshippers who want to say *tarawih* prayers in the evenings.

Muslims in Italy also have a hard time finding places to worship. Muslims need a large amount of floor space to accommodate their prayer rituals, and it is not always easy to find that

◀ Decorative lanterns light the streets for Ramadan outside a mosque in Amsterdam, the Netherlands.

kind of space in Italy. Islamic groups that try to rent halls are sometimes refused by landlords who do not want Islamic events held on their property. The Islamic community is still fairly new to Italy, and Italian people have not yet learned to accommodate Muslims in the way that France and the United Kingdom have. Nevertheless, the Italian government has recently promised to provide the Islamic community with space for its prayers by, for example, converting unused schools into mosques. The government has also tried to encourage Italians to respect Muslims and their beliefs, leaving parking spaces available for Muslims near mosques, for example. The Vatican, the head of the Roman Catholic Church, has even called on Christians to fast during the last Friday of Ramadan in order to demonstrate solidarity with Muslims.

MUSLIMS GO ONLINE IN THE NETHERLANDS

Most of the Muslims in the Netherlands are of Turkish or Moroccan origin. Those who have lived their entire lives in Europe rely on Web sites on Islam and Ramadan to learn about their religious traditions. These Web sites also provide important practical information, such as the day on which Ramadan will begin, the time of sunset and sunrise on a particular day, and locations of mosques within the Netherlands. Some Web sites answer questions about Ramadan posed by both Muslims and non-Muslims. Web sites also conduct polls to gather information about Ramadan practices, such as the percentage of Dutch Muslims who fast during the month. Information is posted in Dutch, which many Muslims in the Netherlands understand better than Arabic.

SHOPS STOCK UP ON POPULAR MUSLIM FOODS IN SPAIN

Many of Spain's Muslims live in the southern part of the country, near Morocco from which many of them emigrated. During the days leading up to Ramadan, shops in southern Spain rush to bring in foods that Muslims eat during the month. Shops are filled with burlap sacks of dates, dried apricots, figs, prunes, nuts, and meat that has been certified *halal*, meaning permissible for Muslims to eat. Many restaurants serve a Moroccan soup called *harira* early in the evenings because it is traditional for Muslim Moroccans to break their fast with this thick, hearty dish.

Spain's larger cities, such as Barcelona and Madrid, have large Islamic communities that tend to concentrate in particular neighborhoods. These areas often resemble Islamic cities during Ramadan with their sacks of dried fruits and nuts on display.

▲ Muslims in Madrid, Spain celebrate Eid Al-Fitr, which marks the end of the month of Ramadan. As of 2015, there were approximately 1.9 million Muslims in Spain, or 4 percent of the population.

TEXT-DEPENDENT QUESTIONS

1: Who was Josip Broz Tito?

2: Name a food that might be found in a German bakery during Ramadan.

3: Approximately how many Muslims live in Italy?

RESEARCH PROJECTS

1: Research the modern history of Muslim migration to Europe, including major waves of migration (such as after World War II) and the recent increase of refugees fleeing war-torn countries and violent political regimes. Create a brief report summarizing your findings. Include a timeline of major events if possible.

2: Research the musical traditions of Islam, including varying ideas about music and its role in the life and worship of Muslims, elements of Islamic music, and the role of poetry and dance in musical expression. Write a brief summary of your findings.

Observing in the Middle East

The Middle East is home to the largest concentration of Muslims in the world. Islam originated in Saudi Arabia and spread quickly throughout the region. Today, about one-fifth of the world's Muslims live in the Middle East. The population of most Middle Eastern nations is almost entirely Islamic, and many of these countries have Islamic governments. Ramadan is a national event in Middle Eastern countries. Nearly everyone participates, whether they want to or not. They fast, they pray, and they celebrate.

■ Ramadan in the Middle East

Ramadan dominates schedules in the Middle East. Schools may start late. Restaurants close during the day and open in the evenings. Shopping malls also close during the day but stay open from 5 P.M. until nearly dawn (they stay open latest during the last 10 days

WORDS TO UNDERSTAND

Compatriots: Two or more people from the same country.
Subdued: Mellow, quiet, or restrained.
Tuber: A structure on a plant used to store nutrients and produce new growth.

◀ A woman and her son sell bread at the Ramadan bazaar in Cairo, Egypt.

RISING AND SETTING WITH A BANG

In many parts of the Middle East, cities fire cannons to mark sunrise and sunset. Other places set off fireworks.

of Ramadan). Even doctors and dentists may have odd hours, offering patients midnight appointments. Because of this, many foreigners find it easiest simply to adopt the Ramadan schedule themselves.

Ramadan is a time for religious study and investigation. Religious leaders in many countries preach special sermons every afternoon and evening during the month. Prayer cycles during Ramadan are particularly long, and it can take an hour or more to perform each of the five daily prayers. During the last 10 days of Ramadan, the period known as Laylat al-Qadr, some mosques hold all-night prayer services at which worshippers spend hours standing at attention and prostrating themselves on the floor. Some worshippers sleep in the mosques toward the end of Ramadan. Shii Muslims hold all-night prayer gatherings in their homes.

In many parts of the Middle East, the sexes do not mingle in public. Often only men attend prayers at mosques. Women say their prayers at home, in private. In other places, men pray downstairs in mosques and women pray upstairs or in separate rooms within the mosque.

Not every Muslim considers Ramadan a time of austerity. Most Middle Eastern Muslims observe Ramadan by fasting during the day and saying special prayers, but at night many people go out and stroll through shopping malls and bazaars for hours.

Although many years ago Ramadan was a time for people to fast, pray, and try to improve themselves, during the 1990s and early 2000s the holiday became much more commercialized. In many Arab cities, Ramadan is celebrated with shopping sprees and all-night parties. Car manufacturers use Ramadan as an occasion to advertise special deals.

During Ramadan, restaurants and hotels set up large tents where people can relax and smoke water pipes all night long. Some of these tents are extremely elaborate. Although they are designed to resemble old Middle Eastern desert tents, they are air conditioned, covered with Persian rugs, and full of modern amenities. Entrance fees are high, from $50 to $100 per person.

Some Middle Eastern nations take fasting during Ramadan extremely seriously. Although non-Muslims are not required to fast while living in or visiting Islamic nations, in some places visitors are strongly advised not to eat or drink in public. Fasting is the most important act of Ramadan and everyone who can fast does fast. At the same time, Ramadan is also an occasion for feasting. Within homes, people prepare many dishes for the evening *iftar* meals. In many villages or neighborhoods in Egypt, Turkey, and other Middle Eastern countries, women compete to make the best food during Ramadan. Neighbors and relatives regularly visit one another during this time. Many women strive to make their most special meals of the year, so they can impress their guests at fabulous *iftar* parties in the evenings. Some religious leaders encourage women to stop cooking so much in order to give themselves more time for prayer. Throughout the Middle East, women are the main household cooks. Depending on the region, women may not be allowed to go out to the market to do the shopping, which can complicate the cooking and dining arrangements.

■ Eid al-Fitr in the Middle East

When the Sun sets on the last day of Ramadan, Muslims throughout the Middle East begin celebrating. They may set off fireworks or shoot cannons. Large cities become clogged with traffic

▲ Shoppers stroll through a display of traditional Ramadan lamps in a bazaar in Cairo, Egypt.

as people run out to shop for last-minute items for their Eid feasts. Eid celebrations can last for several days.

■ Unique Customs and Traditions

LANTERNS IN EGYPT

In Egypt food prices increase by 30 percent as soon as Ramadan starts, and the poor are hit hardest. Charities collect contributions from the wealthy during the months before Ramadan, and use it to buy dried foods such as rice, lentils, pasta, nuts, dried fruit, and sugar, as well as oil for cooking. They then distribute the food to the needy.

Before Ramadan begins, Egyptians buy *yamishramadan*, a selection of dried fruits and nuts to have on hand for the month of fasting. Desserts are very popular; these include baklava, nut and cheese pastries, and pastries made of shredded wheat and honey or sugar syrup. Also popular are sweet drinks, such as an apricot drink called *kamr el din* and a sweet white drink made from the **tubers** of orchid flowers called *salep*.

Some Egyptian Muslims celebrate Ramadan with shopping sprees and all-night parties. Hotels and restaurants in Egypt advertise festive Ramadan meals. Egyptian advertising companies run sweepstakes that promise prizes to anyone who reads their advertisements for all 30 days of Ramadan. Politicians campaigning for office hand out traditional Ramadan lanterns called *fanoos* that are decorated with their names. In Egypt, Muslims use these lanterns to decorate for Ramadan. They hang them from their balconies and in the streets. Most of these lanterns are made of tin cut from old tin cans and colored glass. Candles inside the lanterns provide light. Egyptian children are allowed to stay up late during Ramadan, visiting friends and awaiting the predawn *suhur* meal. They walk through the streets carrying lanterns and singing a traditional Ramadan song, hoping that adults who hear them will give them nuts or candy.

Egyptian Muslims start preparing for Eid several days before the end of Ramadan, baking special Eid cookies–spice cookies that are rolled in sesame seeds or stuffed with dates and nuts and covered in powdered sugar–that they will share with relatives and friends on the holiday. Fish is the heart of many Egyptian Eid meals. Women cook the fish and the rest of the meal in the morning while men go to the mosque.

ALI'S DEATH IS MOURNED IN IRAN

To Shii Muslims the 21st day of Ramadan is a particularly holy day. They believe that in the year 661, Prophet Muhammad's son-in-law Ali was struck on the head while praying on the 19th

▲ A resort in Doha, Qatar is lit up for a Ramadan party. Though most Muslims are **subdued** by day during Ramadan, at night, many party.

day of Ramadan; two days later, he died. Because Shiis believe that Ali was the rightful heir to Muhammad, the anniversary of his death is a very solemn occasion for them. Almost every business in Iran's capital city, Tehran, closes. All television news announcers dress in black. The television and radio programs are devoted to prayers and coverage of Ali's life and his death. Throughout

the country, Muslims gather in same-sex groups (men and women do not mix publicly in Iran) to mourn Ali's death and pray to him. People hire singers to perform sad songs and help them pray for favors from Ali. These performances sometimes move listeners to tears. Many families choose this occasion to cook vast amounts of food to feed their poorer neighbors. They carry the food out into the streets and deliver it to the hungry.

DIFFERENT SCHEDULES FOR SUNNIS AND SHIIS

Iran's Muslims include both Sunnis and Shiis. The majority is Shii. Often these groups start and end Ramadan on different days.

Iran is the big exception to the tradition of celebrating Eid al-Fitr with festivities. In Iran, Eid is a day for special prayers at the mosque and self-congratulation for accomplishing the month of fasting. Iranians do break the fast with family meals, but these tend to be small and private. Iranians do not have the same tradition of festive dishes that other Islamic nations have.

DEPENDING ON CHARITY IN IRAQ

Iraq has been in a state of war since March 2003, with significant tension between Sunni and Shii Muslims and Kurds. Previously, Iraqis celebrated Ramadan much like Muslims in the rest of the Middle East. Women would stock up on food before the month began so that they could prepare traditional specialties such as roast chicken, lamb kebabs, and lentil soup. During the month, families would gather every evening to linger over long meals and then walk together in the dark cities, greeting friends and neighbors well into the night. Men would visit teahouses where they would play dominoes and backgammon. On Eid al-Fitr people would eat a breakfast of bread with honey and buffalo cream (made from the milk of water buffalo). Later in the day they might sacrifice and cook a lamb. For dessert, people would eat date-filled pastries called *klaicha*.

Since the war began, however, Iraqis have had to curtail their Ramadan celebrations. Many people living in the country have no money to buy food and do not feel safe leaving their homes to visit the mosques. In Baghdad, Iraq's capital, curfews keep people inside after dark. Some Iraqi Muslims attempt to reconcile their differences for the sake of the holiday. One Sunni mosque in Baghdad offered free *iftar* meals to all Muslims during Ramadan in 2007. Sunnis and Shiis both lined up with pots in their hands to collect a meal of lentils, chicken, and rice, which they carried home. For many Iraqis, this charity was the only way for them to have Ramadan meals with their families.

DOME OF THE ROCK IN ISRAEL

Every year some 200,000 Muslims visit Jerusalem during Ramadan to pray at the Temple Mount, or Haram al-Sharif. Muslims believe that Muhammad journeyed to heaven from the Dome of the Rock, a temple built on the site. Muhammad is supposed to have said that one prayer from Jerusalem is worth more than 1,000 prayers made elsewhere.

AMIR SPEAKS IN KUWAIT

Kuwait's government runs a charitable and informational organization called the Zakat House that organizes activities throughout Kuwait and in other Islamic and Arabic countries. It is most active during Ramadan, assisting low-income families, providing food for *iftar* and Eid al-Fitr

▲ A Lebanese woman reads the Quran, Islam's holy book, over the graves of her loved ones. Many Muslims visit family graves during the last days of Ramadan.

meals, hosting banquets for the poor, and buying new clothing for orphans. The Zakat House also helps other charitable organizations decide how to use their funds, runs a daily radio program that answers listeners' questions about Kuwait and Islam, and broadcasts religious edicts on *zakat* during Ramadan.

In Kuwait, often Muslims spend Ramadan visiting family and friends. Many of them stay out every night socializing until the Sun comes up. On one evening during the last 10 days of Ramadan the amir, or ruler, of Kuwait traditionally addresses the nation. This event is eagerly awaited by the Kuwaiti people.

VISITING GRAVES IN LEBANON

During Ramadan the streets of Beirut in Lebanon are festooned with Ramadan lights and signs advertising sales in shops. At Ramadan's end, they eat *maamoul*, pastries filled with dates or candied nuts. On the morning of Eid al-Fitr, Lebanese Muslims get up early and rush to

View a Ramadan family feast in Lebanon.

the cemeteries before dawn. Tradition holds that the dead expect their families to visit at that time. The living spend the predawn hour erecting arches of braided palm fronds over the graves and placing bundles of myrtle branches on the graves while chatting with one another and reading the Quran. This tradition is said to date back to the time of Muhammad.

DESERT PICNICS IN OMAN

Hundreds of thousands of Muslim Asians, many of them from Malaysia and Brunei, live and work in Oman. For many of them, Ramadan in the Middle East is a treat. Although it can be hard to find the Southeast Asian foods they like and they miss gatherings with their extended families back home, Malaysian Muslim workers find a sense of community in the Middle East. Southeast Asian families take turns hosting *iftar* meals for their **compatriots**. They also may enjoy eating Middle Eastern foods, such as the many varieties of excellent dates available in the region.

▲ A bakery in Beirut, Lebanon is piled high with special sweets in preparation for Eid a-Fitr.

In Oman during Ramadan, most shops and restaurants, including fast food restaurants, are closed during the day. Bars and nightclubs remain closed for the entire month. In the oil fields in the desert of Oman, people sometimes eat their Ramadan meals on mats laid on the ground. Just before sunset, workers will lay out dates and *laban*, a sour yogurt drink, on a mat in front of the mosque to be enjoyed as a quick snack right after the Sun sets. After evening prayers, they eat a meal that can include mutton (sheep), camel meat, and a bread and milk pudding called *umm ali*. Oil companies also run dining halls for workers that stay open until the early morning during Ramadan.

GARANGAO IN QATAR

The entire country of Qatar gives itself over to Ramadan. Almost all restaurants are closed, and the workday is shortened for the entire month, sometimes by half. Many people take the last 10 days off from work. This is a popular time for Qataris to make their pilgrimage to Mecca. In addition, devout Muslims try to achieve a spiritual purification during Ramadan. Instead of gorging themselves at night, they eat as little as possible to get by. Believers report that the practice becomes easier toward the end of the 30 days and that they feel freed from their negative feelings and anger.

In Qatar the 15th day of Ramadan is a special event called Garangao. In the evening, children dress in their best clothes and visit their relatives and friends, who give them candy. In Qatar the clothes are traditional–girls wear colorful dresses and black headscarves trimmed with gold, and boys wear robes called *thobes* with embroidered vests and caps. The women of the houses prepare little gift bags for the children; in burlap sacks they mix peanuts, walnuts, almonds, raisins and other dried fruits, and candies. In the center of each bag is placed a coin or a small present, often a ceramic figurine. Before the children go out, they sing the Garangao song to the adult members of the family; then they head out in groups to collect their treats, singing to the adults at each house they visit. At the end of the evening, children compare their treats with one another.

Qataris spend five days celebrating Eid. They eat large amounts of food, visit friends and relatives, and go shopping to take advantage of seasonal sales. Children enjoy special events and activities, such as amusement park rides and games. After the festivities end, many people in Qatar choose to fast for an additional 10 days to gain extra spiritual benefits.

STRICT ADHERENCE TO RELIGIOUS RULES IN SAUDI ARABIA

Saudi Arabia's government is strictly Islamic. The Interior Ministry of Saudi Arabia asks non-Muslims not to eat, drink, or smoke where any Muslim can see them during Ramadan. The ministry has threatened to deport any non-Muslim who breaks this rule.

▲ Children in traditional dress head for the toy market with their parents in celebration of Eid al-Fitr.

DRESSING FOR RAMADAN IN SAUDI ARABIA

Both men and women in Saudi Arabia wear a kind of robe called a *thobe*. During Ramadan, Saudi women often dress in fancy *thobes* with heavy embroidery and beading. They may also carry with them prayer beads made of crystal or pearl, both as a prayer aid and as a fashion statement.

In Saudi Arabia men and women are strictly separated. Many houses have separate entrances and living rooms for men and women. When close relatives visit, men and women may occupy the same room, but otherwise women stay in their own quarters. In addition, since 1932 Saudi women have not been allowed to drive cars. Because women are the main household cooks, this can complicate shopping for food for Ramadan and Eid meals. In 2008, the Saudi government announced that women would be allowed to drive, but it will be many years before women are driving in large numbers.

A popular Ramadan food in Saudi Arabia is *samosa*, a small fried pastry filled with meat, cheese, or dates. A typical *iftar* meal will include dates, a yogurt drink called *laban* or fruit juice, soup, *samboosa* (pastries filled with meat or cheese stuffing), *foul* (mashed beans), and a type of bread called *tameez*.

In Saudi Arabia, mosques host free *iftar* meals every night; volunteers donate homemade food and drinks. Many people get up very early and bring meals to the mosques with them so that they can share breakfast after morning prayers. Everyone works together to clean up the mess from this meal.

During the day, Saudis chew a stick called *miswak*, a type of natural toothbrush that can prevent tooth decay and improve breath. Muslims believe that prayers are more effective if they chew *miswak* beforehand.

DINING OUT IN SYRIA

The daily schedule in Damascus, the capital of Syria, follows the same pattern throughout the month of Ramadan. People sleep late and businesses open around noon. During the afternoons, pedestrians and cars begin to move around. Traffic gets worse and food stores get increasingly crowded until sunset. At that point, all the people disappear from the streets and Damascus becomes very quiet while everyone performs their evening prayers and eats their *iftar* meal. About two hours later, however, all the people emerge from their homes and the shops open again. Crowds gather around pastry shops enjoying desserts. Most people go home around midnight to catch a quick rest, but others stay out until *imsak*, the start of fasting, arrives again. At this point a man called a *musaher* walks through the streets beating a drum and admonishing everyone to wake up and eat before the sunrise. Then the revelers go home and rest until late in the morning.

In Syria, family ties become more important during Ramadan. Extended families try to eat several *iftar* meals together, with each household taking a turn to host the whole group. After a meal in a home, people will relax for several hours chatting, smoking water pipes, and playing backgammon.

Some people go out to restaurants for *iftar* meals, but they must make reservations several days in advance. In the most fashionable restaurants it is nearly impossible to get a table during Ramadan. Modern Syrians love restaurants and support many of them. Damascus, for example, is now home to a plethora of trendy restaurants with names such as "Oxygen" and "Neutron." Restaurants serve both traditional Syrian dishes—hummus and pita bread, for example—as well as international food. The popular Oxygen restaurant has a Western menu and draws crowds of diners who often linger over their meals until three or four in the morning.

STREET FESTIVAL IN TURKEY

During Ramadan, the mosques and streets in Turkey are decorated with colored lights. Vendors set up booths on the sidewalks and in squares in the evenings and sell snacks, toys, and religious items. Many Turks are not devout Muslims and do not fast during the day, but they nevertheless participate in the evening feasts with their more religious friends and relatives. In Turkey almost every Ramadan table includes *samboosa*, pastries filled with meat or cheese, soup called *shurba*, spaghetti, and *shafoot*, a mix of bread, milk, and greens. When a Turk visits a household for an evening meal, he or she greets the family members with kisses and the phrase "Allah Kabul Etsin," which means "may God accept." Though not many fast for Ramadan, towns and cities in Turkey do organize fund-raisers for the less fortunate. On Eid al-Fitr, children go around the neighborhood wishing everyone a happy holiday and collecting candy or money.

Turkey is home to a community of several million people of a faith called Alevi, a Shii group with a traditionally strong dedication to Ali. Alevis believe that men and women are equal and can pray together. Alevi women are not required to wear headscarves. Worshippers perform whirling dances during religious services as well as singing mystical songs. They are tolerant toward other religious beliefs. Alevis do not pray in mosques, though they do go on pilgrimages to Mecca. They

▲ Women shop in Istanbul, Turkey, on the first day of Eid al-Fitr.

do not give *zakat* alms, though most Alevis do donate food and money to charity during Ramadan. Alevis do not believe that they must fast during Ramadan, which causes problems for them in predominantly Islamic areas. Other Muslims tend to be suspicious of Alevis. Some Alevis fast anyway at work and school because of pressure from Muslims.

TENTS IN THE UNITED ARAB EMIRATES

During Ramadan in Dubai, the capital city of the United Arab Emirates, friends and relatives send Ramadan greeting cards to one another. Businesses and houses are decorated with colorful lights, and the television and newspapers are full of advertisements for holiday sales. Some companies spend half their yearly advertising budget during Ramadan. Shopping malls stay open all night long and run contests offering late-night shopping sprees. These malls often set up elaborate Ramadan displays featuring moving models of camels, desert scenes with tents, and live village elders who read traditional stories. Muslims celebrating the month hold all-night parties in tents that they set up in the desert. Residents of Dubai vie to get into the most fashionable hotel tents to spend their Ramadan evenings. They look up reviews of events on Web sites to see which are the best to visit. Many people spend the entire night from *iftar* to *sahur* in the tent, smoking water pipes, drinking coffee, and eating delicacies.

In Dubai, charitable organizations also set up tents that serve *iftar* meals to workers. Many foreign workers cannot afford the high prices that are common in the city and they do not have families living in the country, so they line up to get free meals at the tents. These tents can become very crowded with people trying to get free food, much of it donated by wealthy Muslims. Meals in these tents are fairly simple, consisting of dates, rice, meat, salad, and water. These events make it easier for workers missing their families to get through the holiday season.

Religious leaders complain that Ramadan has become a commercial holiday, much the way some Christian religious leaders complain about the commercialization of Christmas. They object that the people of Dubai have transformed the holiday into a monthlong shopping spree. Leaders urge their believers to focus on the spiritual side of Ramadan instead of worldly matters such as shopping. Some Muslims also complain about the extravagance of the month and the difficulty of finding the spiritual meaning of Ramadan amid all the shopping and feasting.

FIRING CANNONS IN YEMEN

During Ramadan Yemenis often watch religious programs on television and ask religious leaders for advice on spiritual matters. Every large city in Yemen has a cannon, dating from Turkish occupation more than 100 years ago; these cannons are fired every evening to announce the end of the day's

▲ People mingle at one of the many tables set up at a community iftar. From plain white charity tents set up by local mosques to glitzy marquees, Dubai comes alive at night during Ramadan.

fast. Every afternoon before sunrise people listen for the sound of the cannon. Children gather around the cannons and beg the men in charge to fire them. Once the fast is broken, almost every Ramadan table in Yemen includes *samboosa*, pastries filled with meat or cheese; a soup called *shurba*; spaghetti; and *shafoot*, a mix of bread, milk, and greens. In Yemeni cities, shops stay open all night long during Ramadan, closing only at sunrise. Women go out in the evenings to buy clothing for themselves and their children; many shops offer sales during Ramadan. People then go home and sleep through the morning.

TEXT-DEPENDENT QUESTIONS

1: In what Middle Eastern country did Islam originate?

2: Why is the 21st day of Ramadan a particularly holy day to Shii Muslims?

3: Where is the Zakat House organization located, and what does it do?

RESEARCH PROJECTS

1: Research the Egyptian holiday of Sham el Nessim, or "Sniffing the Breeze." Write a brief report about what this holiday is, when it takes place, and how it is celebrated.

2: Research the sacred site of the Temple Mount, including its history, location, and significance to Jews, Christians, and Muslims. Write a brief report summarizing your findings.

Observing in North America

Since the late 1980s, hundreds of thousands of Muslims have immigrated to the United States and Canada. Most immigrants are continuing their faith and raising their children as Muslims. Some non-Muslim North Americans have also converted to Islam. Many of these Muslims observe Islamic religious practices, including the month of Ramadan. Muslims living in North America do their best to keep Ramadan traditions alive even though many of them feel isolated and miss the larger Islamic communities of their homelands. Even those who live in Islamic neighborhoods in major cities such as New York and Toronto may miss the specific atmosphere and traditions of their own countries. They therefore go out of their way to greet fellow Muslims when they recognize them with an enthusiastic "Ramadan Mubarak!"

WORDS TO UNDERSTAND

Assimilation: The process of adapting one's attitudes and customs to a new culture.

Solidarity: Mutual support among people with common interests, purposes, or concerns.

Stereotype: A fixed set of oversimplified ideas that people think represent a wide group of people.

◀ Muslims celebrate the completion of Ramadan at the Central Florida Fairgrounds in Orlando.

Each year, the Fiqh Council of North America makes the official announcement of the day on which Ramadan begins, based on word from Islamic scholars and astronomers that the new Moon is visible. The astronomers consult the U.S. Naval Observatory's statements about the state of the Moon, but they rely more on their own observation of the sky. Once the scholars have agreed that the new Moon is visible, the Islamic Society of North America announces the start of Ramadan on its Web site, prompting religious leaders and individual Muslims all across North America to begin the fast.

▲ Dates, water, and milk are shared with Muslims and passersby during the first public iftar in Montreal, Canada in 2016.

■ Ramadan in Canada

As of 2011, there were over 1 million Muslims living in Canada, most of them very recent immigrants. Within the past generation, Canada has seen the construction of many mosques and Islamic schools, and the institution of large-scale public prayers. Toronto is home to about 200 mosques and prayer rooms. About 60,000 Muslims live in the capital city of Ottawa. Canada's Muslims come from all over the world, and they bring their native Ramadan traditions to their celebrations in Canada. Though Canadian Muslims face similar challenges of **assimilation** as their American neighbors to the south, the international climate of the country's major cities helps ease their transition. They can seek out not only other Muslims but also others of common ethnic background. Middle Eastern, Caribbean, and African Islamic communities are all represented in various cities throughout Canada, making Ramadan a time of both religious **solidarity** and diverse cultural exchange.

OTTAWA

Ottawa is the capital of Canada and has a very cosmopolitan atmosphere. As such, Ramadan celebrations are a mixture of secular and sacred traditions. In the evenings people will congregate at mosques to pray and then relocate to various schools, universities, or auditoriums to share their *iftar* meal. As in the United States, a different ethnic Muslim community hosts the meal each evening. Following the meal, there is often a less traditional activity such as a lecture, film, or poetry reading that incorporates the lessons of Ramadan. The organizers of these events hope that they will foster a dialogue on the nature of Ramadan as well as the role of Islam in modern life. With Ottawa's role as a political center, it is not uncommon to see people of all nationalities and backgrounds taking part in these activities and participating in ensuing discussions.

Hear a prayer for Eid al-Fitr in Ottawa.

TORONTO

On Eid al-Fitr, thousands of Toronto's Muslims gather for prayers at the Canadian National Exhibition. The event is advertised as "Canada's Largest Eid Prayer." The event has drawn more

WHAT WESTERN MUSLIMS WEAR

American and Canadian Muslims wear a variety of clothing styles. Muslims born in North America usually wear Western clothes, while first-generation immigrants often wear the clothing of their native countries. Sometimes they combine elements from different Islamic nations. For example, a woman might wear a Turkish-style headscarf with Indian-style loose pants and long shirt. A young man might wear an Arab headdress called a *kaffiyah* with a Western-style suit.

than 15,000 Muslims in the past. The prayer takes place in the morning, and is followed by games and a bazaar where people can celebrate the holiday by shopping, eating, and socializing.

WINNIPEG, MANITOBA

As of 2011, there were over 11,000 Muslims living in Winnipeg, Manitoba. On Eid al-Fitr, most of these believers gather in one place to say Eid prayers. Afterward the group holds a festival for children, concerts, and a large celebratory meal.

■ Ramadan in the United States

Today about 3.3 million Muslims live in the United States. Some longtime Muslim residents of the United States remember that back in the 1970s there were only a handful of Muslims in their towns. Now many cities have Muslim populations of several thousand. For example, about 300,000 Muslims live in southeast Michigan. The Detroit suburb of Dearborn has such a large Arab population that shops and restaurants post signs in Arabic.

September 11, 2001, is a date that holds tremendous significance to Muslims living in North America. On that day, 19 Muslim terrorists hijacked four commercial passenger jets and crashed three of them into specially chosen targets—the two towers of the World Trade Center in New York City and the Pentagon in Washington, D.C. The fourth airplane crashed in rural Pennsylvania. Nearly 3,000 victims died in these attacks, including several hundred firefighters and New York City police officers and transit officers who attempted to save people trapped in the towers in New York.

The terrorists who launched these attacks were affiliated with the radical Muslim group al-Qaeda, an organization of militant Sunni Muslims dedicated to creating a new Muslim empire and getting rid of all foreign influences in Islamic nations. The terrorists supposedly had several aims in

▲ The Muslim community in New York City hosts an outdoor iftar dinner.

attacking the United States on September 11. They hoped to get U.S. troops to leave Saudi Arabia and other parts of the Middle East. They wanted to end U.S. support for Israel. In addition, they believed that it was their religious duty to kill Americans, and they were convinced that if they died for their cause they would be rewarded in heaven.

The people of the United States were understandably shocked and appalled by the September 11 attacks. Americans found it terrifying to think that such attacks could happen in their own country. People around the world

A JEWISH-MUSLIM CONNECTION

Muslims are allowed to eat food that has been certified kosher by a Jewish rabbi. The slaughtering methods are similar, so kosher food counts as *halal*.

condemned the al-Qaeda terrorists. Unfortunately, many Americans drew the false conclusion that all Muslims were terrorists. Frightened by the attacks and frustrated by their inability to protect themselves, some Americans lashed out at Middle Eastern people and people who looked as if they might be Muslim. Many Muslims said they had been verbally attacked by Americans who called them terrorists. American Muslims found it very difficult to live in America just after the 9-11 attacks.

Even years later, American Muslims say that they feel life in the United States is harder for them than it was before 2001. The vast majority of Muslims living in the United States reject Islamic extremism and condemn acts of terrorism. A number of them are very concerned about the rise of radical Islam. They complain, though, that many Americans do not realize this and prefer to judge them based on **stereotypes**. One big problem that many Muslims see is that Americans do not know much about Islam. Many young Muslims in the United States want to educate Westerners about their religion to convince people that Islam is not a religion of terrorists.

Though such cross-cultural exchanges can lead to grave misunderstandings, America's rich diversity is more often an advantage to the celebration of Ramadan. Many American Muslims eat Ramadan meals at home, often inviting non-Muslim friends to join them. Mosques usually offer multicultural *iftar* meals during Ramadan. Each night the mosques furnish holiday meals in the style of a different country. One night the food might be Moroccan. The next night immigrants from India might cook their native food. Over the course of the month, diners might sample food from Afghanistan, Bosnia, Thailand, China, and Egypt. Some Muslims eat only food that is *halal*, or permissible, meaning that it has been prepared in a particular way that conforms to Islamic laws.

CHRISTIANS FASTING WITH MUSLIMS

Some United States Christians fast during Ramadan to show solidarity with Islam and as a spiritual offering to God.

Muslims are not allowed to eat pork, and the animals they eat are supposed to be slaughtered in a particular way. In the late 1980s it was difficult for Muslims to find *halal* food; now *halal* food items are readily available in many cities throughout the United States. Some company cafeterias have begun offering *halal* meals to their employees as well. Because it is hard to know for sure if food in restaurants is *halal*, many Muslims avoid breaking religious rules by eating vegetarian when they go out. However many American Muslims do not worry about *halal* rules.

A TIGHT-KNIT COMMUNITY IN DEARBORN, MICHIGAN
Warren Avenue in Dearborn is a haven for Muslims living in this Michigan city. It is lined with shops selling delicacies dear to Middle Easterners—Arabic books, hookahs (special pipes used to smoke flavored tobacco), pastries made with nuts and honey, and *halal* meat. Muslims, many of the women wearing headscarves, like to congregate there to buy their favorite foods, including

▲ A group of women shared ice cream and a deep-fried Twinkies to celebrate Eid Al-Fitr, which marks the end of Ramadan, at the Minnesota State Fair in St. Paul.

shish kebabs (pieces of meat and vegetables cooked on skewers), spicy potatoes, lentil and chickpea soup, and *fattouche*, a Lebanese salad made with torn pieces of toasted pita bread. They may eat these foods at cafés found on the avenue to be social or carry them home for the evening meal.

OFF DUTY!

It can be very hard to catch a cab just after sunset during Ramadan because all the Islamic cabbies are praying and eating!

MUSLIMS IN NEW YORK CITY

Schools in New York City, which have a large Muslim population, make some accommodations for their Islamic students during Ramadan. For example, some sports coaches give their Muslim students a break during practice to grab a snack at sunset. School nurses report larger than usual numbers of students fainting or reporting headaches and stomachaches, the results of fasting during the day.

Many taxi drivers in New York City are Muslim. During Ramadan, they often have a supply of snack foods such as dates, so they can grab a quick bite the moment the Sun sets. Some even carry their *iftar* meals in the car. Most cabbies, however, take a break after sunset to pray and eat their *iftar* meal. Many of them congregate in Manhattan's East Side, near the corner of Lexington Avenue and 28th Street, home of a number of restaurants selling the foods of various Islamic nations. Cabbies seeking the taste of their homelands who want something a little more traditional can grab dates, hot tea, curries, chickpea stews, pastries stuffed with meat or potatoes, and any number of other Middle Eastern and South Asian specialties.

TEXT-DEPENDENT QUESTIONS

1: How many Muslims were living in Winnipeg, Manitoba, as of 2011?

2: What is *fattouche*?

3: What is one way that schools in New York City accommodate Islamic students during Ramadan?

RESEARCH PROJECTS

1: Research the twelve months of the Islamic calendar. Create a chart showing each month, the meaning of its name in English, and any noteworthy events or spiritual significance.

2: Research an Islamic cultural center in the United States, such as the Islamic Center of New York, the Islamic Society of Mid Manhattan, or the Islamic Center of Southern California. Write a brief overview of the center, including its history, mission, and any work it does to promote interfaith dialogue.

▲ Iftar meals, breaking the Ramadan fast, are a joyful tradition for Muslim families.

Series Glossary

ancestors The direct family members of one who is deceased

aristocrat A member of a high social class, the nobility, or the ruling class

atonement The act of making up for sins so that they may be forgiven

ayatollah A major religious leader, scholar, and teacher in Shii Islam; the religious leader of Iran

colonial era A period of time between the 17th to 19th century when many countries of the Americas and Africa were colonized by Europeans.

colonize To travel to and settle in a foreign land that has already been settled by groups of people. To colonize can mean to take control of the indigenous groups already in the area or to wield power over them in order to control their human and physical resources.

commemorate To honor the memory of a person or event

commercialization The act of reorganizing or reworking something in order to extract profit from it

descendant One who comes from a specific ancestor

Eastern Orthodox Church The group of Christian churches that includes the Greek Orthodox, Russian Orthodox, and several other churches led by patriarchs in Istanbul (Constantinople), Jerusalem, Antioch, and Alexandria.

effigy A representation of someone or something, often used for mockery

equinox Either of the two times during each year when night and day are approximately the same length of time. The spring equinox typically falls around March 21 and the autumnal equinox around September 23.

fast To abstain from eating for a set period of time, or to eat at only prescribed times of the day as directed by religious custom or law.

feast day A day when a religious celebration occurs and an intricate feast is prepared and eaten.

firsthand From the original source; experienced in person

Five Pillars of Islam The five duties Muslims must observe: declaring that there is only one God and Muhammad is his prophet, praying five times a day, giving to charity, fasting during Ramadan, and making a pilgrimage to Mecca

foundation myth A story that describes the foundation of a nation in a way that inspires its people

Gregorian calendar The calendar in use through most of the world

hedonism The belief that pleasure is the sole good in life

Hindu A follower of Hinduism, the dominant religion of India

imam A leader; a scholar of Islam; the head of a mosque

indigenous Originating in or native to a specific region; often refers to living things such as people, animals, and plants

Islam The religious faith of Muslims. Muslims believe that Allah is the only God, and Muhammad was his prophet

Judaism A religion that developed among the ancient Hebrews. Followers of Judaism believe in one God and follow specific laws written in the Torah and the Talmud, and revealed to them by Moses.

Julian calendar Is named after Julius Caesar, a military leader and dictator of ancient Rome, who introduced it in 46 B.C.E. The Julian calendar has 365 days divided into 12 months, and begins on January 1. An extra day, or leap day, is added every four years (February 29) so that the years will average out to 365.242, which is quite close to the actual 365.242199 days of Earth's orbit.

lower realm In the Asian tradition, the place where the souls end up if their actions on Earth were not good

lunar Related to the Moon

martyr A person who willingly undergoes pain or death because of a strong belief or principle

masquerade A party to which people wear masks, and sometimes costumes or disguises

millennium 1,000 years

monarch A king or queen; a ruler who inherits the throne from a parent or other relative

monotheism The belief in the supremacy of one god (and not many) that began with Judaism more than 4,000 years ago and also includes the major religions of Islam and Christianity.

mosque An Islamic house of worship

mourning The expression of sorrow for the loss of a loved one, typically involving

movable feast A religious feast day that occurs on a different day every year

Muhammad The prophet to whom God revealed the Quran, considered the final prophet of Islam

mullah A clergyman who is an expert on the Quran and Islamic religious matters

Muslim A person who follows the Islamic religion

New Testament The books of the Bible that were written after the birth of Christ

New World A term used to describe the Americas from the point of view of the Western Europeans (especially those from France, England, Portugal, and Spain) who colonized and settled what is today North and South America.

offering Donation of food or money given in the name of a deity or God

Old Testament The Christian term for the Hebrew Scriptures of the Bible, written before the birth of Christ

oral tradition Stories told aloud, rather than written, as a way to pass down history

pagan Originally, someone in ancient Europe who lived in the countryside; a person or group that does not believe in one god, but often believes in many gods that are closely connected to nature and the natural world

pageantry Spectacle, elaborate display

parody Imitation of something, exaggerated for comic effect—for example, a parody of science fiction movies.

patria Fatherland; nation; homeland

peasant People who farm land that usually belongs to someone else, such as a landowner

penance The repentance of sins, including confessing, expressing regret for having committed them, and doing something to earn forgiveness

piety A strong belief in and correspondingly fervent practice of religion

pilgrimage A journey undertaken to a specific destination, often for religious purposes

prank A mischievous or humorous trick

pre-Columbian Of or relating to the period before Christopher Columbus arrived in the Americas

procession A group of people moving together in the same direction, especially in a type of celebration

prophecy A prediction about a future event

prophet An individual who acts as the interpreter or conveyer of the will of God and spreads the word to the followers or possible followers of a religion. A prophet can also be a stirring leader or teacher of a religious group. Capitalized it refers to Muhammad.

Protestant A member of a Christian denomination that does not follow the rule of the pope in Rome and is not one of the Eastern Orthodox Churches. Protestant denominations include Anglicans (Episcopalians), Lutherans, Presbyterians, Methodists, Baptists, and many others.

Quran The holy book of Islam

rabbi A Jew who is ordained to lead a Jewish congregation; rabbis are traditionally teachers of Judaism.

reincarnation The belief in some religions that after a person or animal dies, his or her soul will be reborn in another person or animal; it literally means, "to be made flesh again." Many Indian religions such as Hinduism, Sikhism, and Jainism, believe in reincarnation.

repentance To express regret and ask forgiveness for doing something wrong or hurtful.

requiem A Mass for the souls of the dead, especially in the Catholic Church

revel To celebrate in a joyful manner; to take extreme pleasure

ritual A specific action or ceremony typically of religious significance

sacred Connected with God or religious purposes and deemed worthy of veneration and worship

sacrifice Something given up or offered in the name of God, a deity or an ancestor

shaman A spiritual guide who a community believes has unique powers to tell the future and to heal the sick. Shamans can mediate or cooperate with spirits for a community's advantage. Cultures that practice shamanism are found all over the world still today.

Shia A Muslim sect that believes that Ali, Muhammad's son-in-law, should have succeeded Muhammad as the caliph of Islam; a common sect in Iran but worldwide encompassing only about 15 percent of Muslims

solar calendar A calendar that is based on the time it takes Earth to orbit once around the Sun

solar Related to the Sun

solilunar Relating to both the Sun and Moon

solstice Day of the year when the hours of daylight are longest or shortest. The solstices mark the changing of the seasons–when summer begins in the Northern Hemisphere (about June 22) and winter begins in the Northern Hemisphere (about December 22).

spiritual Of or relating to the human spirit or soul, or to religious belief

Sunni The largest Islamic sect, including about 85 percent of the world's Muslims

supernatural Existing outside the natural world

Talmud The document that encompasses the body of Jewish law and customs

Torah Jewish scriptures, the first five books of the Hebrew scriptures, which serve as the core of Jewish belief

veneration Honoring a god or a saint with specific practices

vigil A period in which a person stays awake to await some event

Vodou A religion rooted in traditional African beliefs that is practiced mostly in Haiti, although it is very popular in the West Indies as well. Outside of Haiti it is called *Vodun*.

Further Resources

■ Books

Islam (Major World Religions). By Michael Ashkar. Published in 2017 by Mason Crest, Broomall, Pa. This volume is one in a series exploring the world's major religious traditions. It examines the history and traditions of the Muslim faith.

The Story of the Holy Prophet Muhammad: 30 Stories for 30 Nights. By Humera Malik. Published in 2017 by Green Key Press, Washington, D.C. Complete your own Ramadan journey by following along with these stories about the founder of Islam.

Ramadan: The Holy Month of Fasting. By Ausma Zehanat Khan. Published in 2017 by Orca Book Publishers, Victoria, British Columbia. An introduction to Ramadan with a special focus on the holiday's spiritual significance.

Islam: A Very Short Introduction. By Malise Ruthven. Published in 2016 by Oxford University Press, Oxford, UK. The revised edition of this compact yet thorough survey of Islam includes new information on changes in the Muslim world in the twenty-first century.

Let's Celebrate: Happy Eid al-Fitr. By Joyce Bentley. Published in 2018 by Wayland Books, New York. Learn all about the "sweet festival" marking the end of Ramadan.

■ Web Sites

Australian Broadcasting Corporation. http://www.abc.net.au/religion/stories/s790151.htm. An overview of Islam in Australia, with links to additional resources.

Hartford Seminary. http://www.hartsem.edu/macdonald-center/information-resources/information-on-islam/. Information on Islamic topics, assembled by a team at Connecticut's Hartford Seminary.

History.com. http://www.history.com/topics/holidays/ramadan. An overview of Islam and Ramadan from the History channel, with video clips.

Islamic Society of North America. http://www.isna.net. Furnishes information of use to North American Muslims.

Salaam.com. http://www.salaam.co.uk. A clearinghouse of Islamic articles, biographies, and news postings.

Timeoutdubai.com. http://www.timeoutdubai.com. A calendar of events in Dubai.

▲ Muslims gather for prayers in a mosque in Jakarta, Indonesia. Men and women traditionally pray on separate sides.

Index

Alevi 76–77

bathing 19, 24
British Muslims 56–57
burqa 24

Canadian National Exhibition 83
Chand Raat (night of the Moon) 47
charity 8, 20, 27, 40, 70, 77
cleanliness 24

Dome of the Rock 70

Eid al-Fitr 6, 8, 14–15, 22–23, 32, 35–36, 44–48,
    50–51, 54–58, 67, 70–71, 76, 83–84

fasting 8, 19–23, 27–28, 32, 36, 40, 43–45, 47,
    51, 54, 56–58, 66, 68, 70, 75, 88
festival of sweets 51
The Fiqh Council 15, 82
Five Pillars of Islam 12–13

Garangao 73
graves, visiting 40, 48, 50, 71–72

hijab 26

iftar meal 21, 28, 38, 41, 54, 56, 58, 66, 70, 72,
    74–75, 77, 83, 86, 88

lanterns 68

Mecca 12, 27, 57, 73, 76
Moon 14–15, 22, 47, 50, 57, 82
Mosques 20, 24, 27, 32, 35, 38, 40, 44–47, 54,
    58, 60–61, 66, 70, 75–76, 83, 86

Night of Decree (Laylat al-Qadr) 16
Night of Power (Shab e-Qadr) 46
night of the Moon 47

pilgrimage 11–12, 73, 76
prayer 8, 13, 15–16, 19–20, 23–24, 27, 32, 38–40,
    44–48, 50, 54, 56–58, 60–61, 66–67, 69–70,
    73–75, 83–84

Quran 12, 14–16, 20, 27, 32, 36, 38, 40–41,
    44–45, 56, 72

ritual postures (*rakah*) 19, 27

seclusion, period of (*itikaf*) 16

Temple Mount 70

Umar ibn al-Khattab 13
Uthman ibn Affan 13

veils 26, 60

women 20, 24, 26, 32, 35, 40, 44–46, 48, 54, 57,
    60, 66–70, 73–74, 76, 79, 87

Zakat House 70–71

Picture Credits